RB 13

NEPAL

NEPAL

The Discovery of the Malla

By GIUSEPPE TUCCI

TRANSLATED FROM THE ITALIAN
BY LOVETT EDWARDS

New York
E. P. DUTTON & CO., INC.

FIRST PUBLISHED IN ENGLISH
IN 1962

First published in the U.S.A. 1962
by E. P. Dutton & Co. Inc.

English translation ©
George Allen & Unwin, Ltd., London, and
E. P. Dutton & Co. Inc., New York, 1962.

Translated from

NEPAL: ALLA SCOPERTA DEI MALLA

© Leonardo da Vinci Editrice, Bari, 1960

PRINTED IN GREAT BRITAIN
in 11 point Juliana
BY EAST MIDLAND PRINTING CO., LTD.
BURY ST. EDMUNDS, SUFFOLK

PREFACE

THIS book is not a diary but a brief account of a journey in one of the least known areas of Nepal, a journey which, because of the results achieved, was one of the most successful of the many I have made in the course of almost thirty years in the Himalayas and on the Roof of the World.

I have already given a preliminary report of the scientific results of this journey in a detailed study written in English and intended for those learned in the history of Asia.* The pages that follow tell briefly of the events of the journey, allude to the discoveries made and their importance, and serve almost as a commentary on the photographic record of Signorina Francesca Bonardi, to whom I entrusted the task of perpetuating in her photographs the peoples, the landscapes and the discoveries.

If I find myself speaking once again of my Himalayan expeditions, it is not owing to the restlessness of a footloose person but rather to the well-considered decision of a man of science. Science, we know, is a continuous shading of certainty into doubt and every advance that it makes is measured not by the light that it sheds but rather by the greater contrast of the zone of shadow that it reveals. It is not therefore surprising if I take up once more an unfinished record begun on another expedition briefly narrated in *Jungles and Pagodas*. During that journey from the crystalline transparency

* G. Tucci. Preliminary report on two scientific expeditions in Nepal. S.O.R. x. 1. Roma. I.S.M.E.O., 1956.

of the Himalayan skies to the borders of Tibet I descended into the jungles of the Terai to the place where, six centuries before Christ, the Buddha was born, to remind men once more that 'evil should never be requited in this world by evil, but evil is requited by good'. The discoveries of that journey served to determine one thing only; that we still know nothing whatever of the history of Nepal. In fact, since researches have been limited to the valley where all the larger cities are situated, all the rest of the country is *terra incognita*. It is as if we knew only the events of Rome and Latium, and all the rest of Italy remained a mystery. The fault, to tell the truth, is not ours alone; Nepal has jealously kept herself closed to outsiders for centuries past, and only a short while ago half-opened her gates to the adventurous spirit of the climbers who gather there from all parts of the world to lower the pride of her magnificent peaks; they break down one by one the myths and fables which admiration and amazement at the silent menace of the peaks have created to explain the inaccessibility of the forbidden dwellings of the gods suspended in the skies.

For my own part, I am quite ready to scale mountains when I find them in my path; naturally, during eight journeys in Tibet and six in Nepal, I have surmounted several, some of them of more than eighteen thousand feet. But the aim of my expeditions has been quite different; that of revealing and preserving, at least insofar as the record of photography may preserve, the remnants of the civilizations which have succeeded one another in the Himalayan area, and of reconstructing the complex events of the peoples who form a bridge between the Indian subcontinent and Central Asia.

Our century, devoted to sport, practical and efficient, runs the risk of forgetting that valleys and mountains are not merely nature, but are also the refuge or retreat of migrations and of peoples. Looked at in this way, exploration is not a descriptive knowledge of physical reality, nor is it a study of the strata which register the travail of creation, nor a search for the riches that the sub-soil conceals from our greed; exploration is above all the revelation of human life and, I would insist, not only in the present. To explore also means to descend into the depths of the past, to retrace with the aid of science and imagination the road of time and to restore to the light the events of the past, to make them once more alive, to justify them and find once more in them the eternal human values. I have been asked what could there be to interest us in Nepal, and I replied: whenever there is one man, one only, there we are too; and where there is a memory of the past there we shall find fresh forms of the same illusions, fresh evidence, different but not discordant, of the basic patterns of the human spirit.

Furthermore, Nepal is not suspended in a void; it is a part of that complex of Asiatic cultures which from the dawn of history has been linked with Europe by enduring bonds and by trade to such an extent that it has created a unity of all the ancient world, which I would call a Euro-Afro-Asiatic unity, woven of invasion and resistance, of trade and of competition, of mutual expansion and withdrawal but, precisely because of its variety and cohesion, its participation or separation, so actively creative that only in this triune continent, diverse and yet united, the greatest adventures of the mind and the imagination have taken place.

When I made up my mind to go on the expedition described in this book I had received uncertain information, garnered from old Tibetan sources or which had reached me in the course of earlier journeys, of the existence in ancient times in western Nepal of independent principalities whose past was lost in obscurity and which had then, little by little, passed under the rule of Prithivi Narayan who, moving down from his castle at Gorkha in the eighteenth century, had for the first time founded the unity and power of Nepal. I now proposed to find out on the spot if such traditions were true, and I hoped to find in the course of my journey some trace or vestige of the past, in books or other evidence, which might throw light on this puzzle. But I never thought that my exploration would be so fruitful, or that an empire which has been completely forgotten would have leapt out of the centuries of silence, with records fragmentary but none the less sufficient to establish the most notable events of its history. And there was indeed such an empire, the empire of the Malla who not only reigned over western Nepal but also over western Tibet and whose existence, so unexpectedly brought to light, completely upsets the ideas to which we have become accustomed. These kings of western Tibet, whom we know from Tibetan historians not to have been Tibetans, were really the Malla who had extended their rule to the north of the Himalayas and, in order to make their rule more acceptable to their Tibetan subjects, were either converted to Buddhism or, if they already practised it, became its most zealous proselytizers. Moreover, since they controlled the Indian pilgrims' way towards Manasarovar and Kailasa and the traffic between India and Tibet, they were certain also to have exploited the rich goldmines of Tok-Jalung.

This discovery seemed to me the more sudden and unexpected because, as will be seen from the account of the journey, we had, marching for many weeks through the most northerly areas on the confines of Tibet, for the most part almost uninhabited save for a few monasteries, the impression of traversing a country where man had never been able to free himself from the terrifying dominance of nature which almost overwhelmed him with her pitiless indifference, the cruelty of her extremes and the emptiness of her solitudes.

Temples, ruins, inscriptions and chronicles came suddenly upon me as if for many centuries they had been awaiting the propitious moment to reveal to me the events of an empire which for three centuries had held sway over a country larger than Italy. That is the real subject of this book.

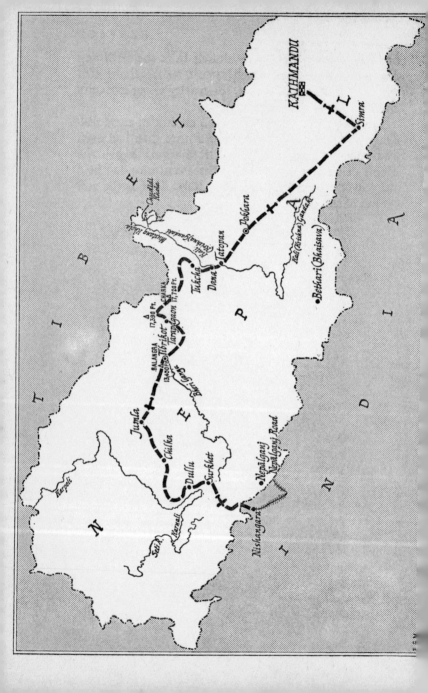

CONTENTS

ILLUSTRATIONS

FROM KATHMANDU TO TUKCHA

In my 1954 expedition, the sixth undertaken in Nepal, my companions were, as usual, not very many; I had with me only Doctor Vito Amorosino, a lieutenant-colonel in the naval medical service, and Signorina Francesca Bonardi. A doctor was necessary because the climate of Nepal, especially in the depths of the valleys, is one of the most pernicious in the world. Dr Guttuso, who came with me on the 1952 expedition, and Dr Amorosino both know this from bitter experience. They saw passing before their eyes a lamentable procession, representing all the plagues and evils of the flesh searching for remedies long valueless because asked for too late.

Signorina Bonardi had the task of recording on film all that we might be able to discover in the course of the journey, since between me and any sort of mechanical apparatus, even a camera, there has always been an absolute incompatibility of understanding. Both of them stood the many fatigues of the journey with great fortitude and obeyed my instructions implicitly.

I demand from my companions not only discipline but above all a prudent and circumspect psychological adaptation to the people, a comprehensive and tender humanity, and a respect for differing customs and habits. No one can accompany me, or at least not without much mutual exasperation, who tries to counter the simplicity, albeit sometimes perverse, of the inhabitants with the presumption of the superiority of his own civilization or of his own religion. In such a case the traveller, despising all that he sees and irritated by it, finds himself overbearing and petulant, in a world that closes itself before him, as certain sensitive plants withdraw into themselves as soon as they are touched.

It is hard to say to what extent recent events may have changed the situation, especially in the interior, but my experience leads me to advise anyone accustomed to lay down his plans in advance to arm himself with much patience. Nepal seemed then to be the country of the unexpected, of the casual, of the uncertain and of the makeshift. Nature and man still seem to enjoy either a capricious liberty or a resigned indolence which throws all foresight to the four winds. Time no longer matters and has a slower rhythm, it is an accident and not a necessity.

The aim of my journey was to study the western provinces of Nepal and especially the area around Jumla. I had therefore made arrangements to leave from Nepalganj, a little frontier town on the edge of the Terai. It is the shortest way, albeit the most unpleasant because of the damp heat and the extraordinary unhealthiness of the area. But on my arrival at Delhi I received my first discouraging reports both from the Nepalese Embassy and from letters which came for me from Kathmandu. The monsoon, which had been more violent than usual and was still at its height, had washed away the few paths closing every access through those districts. I therefore fell back on Kathmandu, imagining that it would be possible to communicate from the capital with the districts of the interior by means of field telephones situated in the principal centres. It was an illusion; there were, in fact, such instruments in one or two places but, as they were dependent on petrol for their power and petrol had to reach them on men's backs from India after many days march, they remained as useless as if they had been broken. The authorities in the capital therefore no longer knew anything whatever of what was going on in the other parts of the country.

Two roads from Kathmandu to Jumla seemed possible; both started from Pokhara. Some old aircraft which were able to land on an improvised airfield linked the capital irregularly with this city, to which strategic factors had given a new importance. Today, the service has become a regular one. From Pokhara the shortest route to Jumla joins the Kali Gandaki river at Baglung, then turns south-west of the Dhaulagiri and then leads into the valley of the Tuliganga at Tarakot and thence onward to Jumla; in the dry season this road is short and easy and does not cross any high passes. The other route passes by Sallyana. But both were closed. All the bridges were down, while floods and landslides had washed away the haphazard paths which nature had designed by chance and which man had followed docilely for centuries. There remained only the road to the north which reaches Jumla by Tukcha and Charka. It had two disadvantages; firstly I would have to retrace for several days an area that I already knew well, that is to say the Pokhara-Tukcha road which I had followed in 1952. Furthermore I would have to cross some very high passes, more than fifteen thousand feet high, which because of the advanced season might be closed at any moment. Since yaks cannot stand up to prolonged or forced marches there was no hope of reaching Charka before the middle of October, which is too late for these very high districts in the heart of the Himalayas. None the less, this itinerary could be of great importance. It passes Tibetan monasteries that the Lamaist *diaspora*, descending through the easiest passes, has scattered south of the Himalayas and runs across a border region

19

where two civilizations and above all two religions, Hinduism and Buddhism, touch one another and, without conflict, merge gently one with the other. It was, therefore, a most suitable terrain for research, provided that the wars which had so often raged in these remote and trackless areas had spared the dwelling-places of the gods. On such journeys one can be sure of nothing; hopes and disappointments are the regular rhythm and, one might almost say, the fascination of adventure. However, there was no other way out and I therefore decided on the Tukcha-Charka-Tarap-Jumla road, incidentally following the advice of a family of merchants who enjoyed great prestige in the Tukcha area and held almost a monopoly of the trade between Upper Nepal and Tibet. They were the Sher Chan, who had already been of great service to me in the expedition of 1952. They found for me a man of trust, the *Sardar* Lal Singh, whose task would be to look after the provisioning and getting together of a new caravan should the first one desert or refuse to continue the march.

The meaning of Nepalese art

For two days the work at Kathmandu was intense. I had to choose the porters and supervise the details of the supplies. I also took on another *sardar*, the Sherpa Pasang, who had taken part in the Everest expedition. He had been chosen especially for me by Tensing who, as everyone knows and as he himself has related in the book dictated to Ullman, was my valued companion in my expedition to Lhasa in 1948.

Lal Singh and Pasang were of entirely different character. Lal Singh was a Newari who stood up very well to fatigue but never took the initiative; he was a timid man, without authority over the caravan men who never troubled to listen to him. During the marches he tried to learn a few words of Italian from Signorina Bonardi, which he painstakingly wrote down in a copybook. What use he could make of them I have never been able to understand. Pasang was a man of quite a different type; ready, quick in action and in making up his mind, and above all energetic and able to find a way out of difficult situations.

We divided the baggage into loads of equal weight, between fifty and sixty pounds, in the hope of reducing to a minimum the inevitable squabbles and discussions on the day of departure. The porters have a very bad habit of competing for the lightest loads and leaving the heavy ones on the ground in the vain hope that others will pick them up.

Kathmandu and the nearby cities, which up to the time when Prithivi Narayan made himself absolute master had been capitals of small states weakened by continual rivalries and petty wars, were centres of a highly developed civilization which spread from these valleys into Tibet. In the eighteenth century the population was made up almost entirely of Newaris, but after the conquest by Prithivi Narayan they were superseded in power by his Gurkhas who boasted of their descent from the warrior tribes of Rajputana. The Newaris through centuries of practice and because of the influence that reached them from India had developed a noble and dignified craftsmanship. Founders of bronze statues, painters able to explain in the symbolism of colour and form the most abstruse complications of mysticism, and patient and imaginative gold- and silversmiths, they became in their turn the teachers of the Tibetans. Naturally, as is usually the case in the East, this art cultivated by the Newaris was above all a religious art. Therefore, if we are to understand its meaning, we must not judge it according to our standards. The Nepalese artists, like

21

their Indian masters or their Tibetan pupils, did not try to give free rein to their imagination in their works. Instead, they translated into the symbolism of certain forms their own experiences and visions, or represented by images and figures the intricate paths through which the initiate must pass in order to transcend the temporal plane and attain the divine and atemporal. Their pictures, wherein the colours do not have a decorative or pictorial value but are fixed by a precise and inviolable symbolism, are like writings in which the elect may read the mystery of things or the intimations of redemption. They are liturgical treatises or mystical visions translated into the calligraphy of line and colour. Certainly, those who can visit one of these temples, be it Buddhist or, which is almost impossible, Hindu, will remain perplexed when faced with certain unfamiliar aspects with which the divine has been made manifest to these men. One is struck by the inhuman indifference; wrapped up in the contemplation of a world to which we are unaccustomed, the countless gods seem not to have eyes or pity for our miseries and our supplications. In most cases also, the aspect in which they are made manifest has nothing human in it, an absurd mingling and co-existence of human and animal forms; heads and arms are multiplied and no standard restrains or moderates the image; the hands brandish weapons and reach out to strike. Other gods, equally monstrous in form, are shown in union with their consorts entwined in ecstasy with the torso of the male. They hold them tightly in their arms, while all around wheel other arms (some have four, six, ten or even more) and above them the terrifying heads threaten, the fanged mouths grin and the eyes seem ready to burst from their sockets in ungovernable fury; they dance upon corpses crushed beneath their immense weight.

But these images are laden with philosophical and liturgical implications. In them is gathered the mystical experience of India, a passion that consumes the world of things and dissolves the personality in an indefinable beginning and end of all creation. These couplings are not erotic insanities but are intended to recall to the initiate that the primaeval androgyne, the ONE who was *in illo tempore* when the universe did not yet exist, is the indivisible union of two opposed yet complementary principles, from whose united labour life springs eternally. The possibility of overcoming time, that is to say death, lies in the recovery of the indivisible ONE. These fearful epiphanies show the warlike aspect of the Divine Mercy which, in order to extirpate the evil which lies in ambush all around, must assume the same demoniacal forms in order to fight with it on equal terms.

The symbols interweave one with the other and combine in a complication of images, bright flashes in the twilit or nocturnal world of the sub-conscious, warning intimations of the savage clash of forces struggling in a universe still chaos and darkness, when the radiance and lightnings are merged in and confounded with the darkness of the murk in tempestuous movement searching desperately for order. But in the serenity of the image of the Buddha or of the god of compassion, Avalokiteshvara, of Padmapani and of Tara, man finds at last the conviction that prayer will not be rejected. He will no longer bow down, abject and terrified, but will pray that the divine and compassionate grace will respond to his plea. If we do not understand the implications of this art it will always remain remote and inaccessible to us. It is only with difficulty therefore that we can appreciate the undeniable formal elegance of some of the images, their power of movement and rhythm in which is reflected the inevitable fact that all experience passes from life to death.

For those who wish to draw closer to the eloquence of Indian art in a spirit of understanding there is nothing more valuable than a visit to the temples of Kathmandu, of Patan and of Bhatgaon, where all the terror, the anguish and the hope of India are expressed with a frankness that approaches exaltation.

At Khatmandu I could not allow myself a moment's rest. Having got the caravan in order, I had to rush to photograph the manuscripts and inscriptions which abound in these cities laden with history. Above all, I had to discuss and dispute with the local learned men who speak Sanskrit as if it were their native language with all the pomposity of doctrine and eloquence but from whom, thanks to this custom, there is much to be learnt since their is no tradition, episode or tale that their prodigious memories do not hold in store and upon which their fertile minds do not comment and embroider.

They confer the illusion of life on a moribund tradition surviving in the palaces of the ancient dynasties and in the temples whose gilded cupolas, smilingly reflecting the sunlight over the weatherbeaten roofs, now grassgrown through lack of attention, seem to want to turn aside any thought of the anguish enclosed within their inviolable chapels.

The crowds throng about them, genuflect and strike the bells to send a message to the gods; but these gods are growing dim.

Too perverse and too remote in their difficult symbolism, they have no compassion for, nor do they alleviate, the resignation and sadness of the faithful. If they are not moved by love, then their absence may become denial. Ascetics, penitents, religious fakirs still

*The stupa, of which this part forms the end,
represents the essential unity of Buddha and the universe;
the eyes show the all-seeingness of Buddha, his identification with the Great All.*

1

2. *The bull, a sacred animal,*
symbol of Shiva,
walks unmolested
in the temple of Pashupati.
Pashupati is one of the many names
of Shiva and is regarded
as the patron or protector
of the whole country.
This temple is therefore
the most noteworthy
of the sacred shrines of Nepal.

3 (overleaf). *The square at Bhatgaon,*
one of the cities which for centuries
were the seat of a local dynasty.
A statue of the king,
in the act of worship,
is on a column facing the temple.

4. *The whole family goes daily to the temple for offerings and prayer. They bring flowers to lay before the gods. There is always a bell, for the worshipper to strike as an act of homage. Music is one of the essential features of the liturgy.*

5. *The corpse of the king's sister is burning on the banks of the Bagmati. Later, the ashes will be collected and scattered in the river. The dying are placed on the rectangular stones, so that they may draw their last breath with their feet in the waters of the river.*

6. *Many-headed
and many-armed images
keep vigil in the silence
of the temples;
here one of the forms of Vishnu
is shown embracing his spouse.*

7 (overleaf). *Vishnu as a wild boar,
in one of his ten avataras
or descents to earth
to liberate it from the prevalence
of demons and of evil.*

8. *Shiva dancing with Parvati.*

9 (overleaf). Terrifying gods, that tear and rend the bodies of the demons or the impious,
keep watch at the entry to the holy places, lest anyone with impure spirit approach them.
This too is one of the incarnations of Vishnu who has taken this form to destroy a demon
that contested the dominion of the universe with the gods.
To carry out this task, Vishnu assumed the guise of a man-lion.

9

swarm in these valleys. But amidst the religious frenzies which are to be seen almost every day in the streets of the cities, the first signs of break-up are already to be seen. Obscure presages are even now hovering in the air. The car that bears in procession the statue of Matsyendranath, one of the most venerated patrons of Nepal, has been broken; golden statues have, with unheard-of sacrilege, been filched from the temples. God-fearing men are beginning to feel that the changes in customs and opinions which have until now been slow in coming are beating impatiently at the gates of the country, which the mountains no longer suffice to isolate from the rest of the world.

Everything indicated worse times ahead if some strong man did not take over the reins of government; the popular view was that only the hereditary crownprince could put an end to the present chaos. He did, in fact, come to the throne in 1955 on his father's death, assuming the name of Mahendra. Nepal was in crisis; the people were protesting against the devaluation of the Nepalese rupee, the lack of stable government, and the incapacity of the politicians, who wasted their time squabbling among themselves or favoured their own relations and supporters while the country headed for disaster. The sick king had to leave for Europe for a cure.

On September 20th I had the equipment for the expedition transported to Pokhara by plane. There would have to be a large number of caravan men, thirty-five porters, since, although I intended to live for a great part of the journey on the resources of the country, for almost a month I would have to cross uncultivated districts which, because of the high altitude, were almost deserted. Medicines naturally took up a great deal of space since we would have to give necessary and humane assistance to the sick, of whom there would certainly be many.

Dr Amorosino made a careful selection of the strongest men, but his task was no easy one since health conditions in Nepal at that time were very poor; malaria and kalazar (black-fever; *Leishmaniosis donovani*) had taken heavy toll of the valleys around Pokhara. Only one out of every six or seven persons whom he examined was considered able to stand the rigours of the journey.

We found Pokhara rather better than it had been in 1952. Some American women-doctors had opened a dispensary, and Indian doctors were doing all in their power to improve the sanitary conditions of the district. But their task was no small one since they had to fight against certain superstitions which resisted with a force more difficult to overcome than that of inertia and local conditions. To succeed in their aim they had first of all to build a hospital, but once this seemed settled the objections began; the Brahmans were resolutely hostile to the proposal because the site had been reserved as a pasture for cows; the cow is sacred and must be treated with the consideration due to sacred things. It is certainly true that at that time in Kathmandu there was (I do not know if it is so now) a large building specially set aside as an alms-house for cows. I do not know if there was then an alms-house for the aged. Things can always be looked at from a different viewpoint in the varied and transient history of man.

We left Pokhara on September 22nd, speeded on our way by the good wishes of my friend Purang Singh, the governor of the province. Instead of the road by Sarang Kot and Kashi Kot, which I had already taken in 1952 and which begins to rise almost at once after leaving Pokhara, I chose the valley road which leads by easy stages to Nodhana. We left in a rainstorm; from then onwards there was scarcely a single day when the rain did not dampen both our bodies and our spirits. The damp fell from the skies, rose from the earth and filled the air; the fury of the waters washed out the last remaining traces of the paths suspended over the abysses and advanced to attack the rocks balanced over the rivers in spate.

From Pokhara we managed to reach the Gandaki river. The bridge there is always dangerous but it was not in such bad repair as we had found it in 1952; we halted in the middle to gaze down at the waters that foamed below and, following the example of the porters, we threw into the gorge the flowers that we had picked on the banks offering them, as is the custom, to the wayward deities of the river.

The road from Pokhara to Tukcha usually takes seven days; we, however, took nine since at Ulleri (6,480 feet) and later at the pass of the same name (9,055 feet) it seemed as if the world had come to an end. We had scarcely got there when the rain poured down in torrents and we were fully exposed as we worked in the vain hope of obtaining timely shelter in the tents. None the less, we rejected the new path carved out, immediately after Dana, by a landslide which had rolled down to the Gandaki river and, holding on by the matted tangle of the creepers, managed to cross safe and sound on what remained of the old path suspended above the waters.

We were more fortunate than those pilgrims who, a few days before, in this very place had fallen into the river below and were never heard of again.

We arrived at Kabu at sunset; the village was made up of a few houses scattered on the mountain side; the fields on the steep slopes between the rocks and the forests were green with barley enclosing the village in a

27

girdle of emerald. There was no level place to pitch our tents and no hope whatsoever that the people would take us into their homes. They were almost all of them orthodox Hindus, Brahmans or Khets, who would not tolerate the contamination of our presence. Luckily, there were also a few Magars. They are more liberal; with only a thin veneer of Hinduism they have to a great extent remained faithful to their former beliefs. One of them took courage and, defying the murmurs of the villagers, opened the doors of his house to us. But there was not room for all of us inside and we had therefore to pitch our tents on the roof, one beside the other. We had to be very careful in our movements since we were so close to the edge that one false step would have been enough to send us tumbling down.

On this road, which I had already passed in 1952, meetings with old acquaintances were not infrequent. Though somewhat shy and reserved, they did not forget those who had treated them with humanity and understanding.

Quite close to Dana, while we were feeling our way cautiously along the slippery and perilous track, passing a caravan which was coming in the opposite direction, I found myself face to face with a woman who recognized me and smiled. I could not recall her, since in this country faces imprint themselves on the memory only with difficulty; to us, everyone seems alike. I halted and remembered where we had met; it was at Baglung in 1952 when she lay dying of a liver attack, and Guttuso, who accompanied me that year, had done all he could to save her. She had passed the night in a hovel close to the camp and the doctor went both morning and evening to attend her. Also we halted there a day longer than we had intended, so as not to desert her.

Buddhism and Hinduism meet

At Tukcha another halt longer than foreseen increased the premonitions instilled in me by the lateness of the season. I would have liked to hasten the timetable, perhaps even to make double marches, and yet here I was still waiting and inactive. None the less I sent home the porters from Pokhara who would not have been able to withstand the cold and the high altitudes where we were going. Their place was taken by yaks, the customary beasts of burden in these parts.

The yak plays a large part in the life of the Tibetans; in ancient times, when they had not yet domesticated it and had to hunt it in dangerous conditions, they considered it a demon. For this reason their autochthonous mythology, before it became mellowed by Buddhism, told of the great deeds of heroes who overcame tremendous and malevolent deities in the form of this animal. Later, they used it as a riding animal and as a beast of burden, made use of its milk and its meat. With its hair they made the tents in which they sheltered during their continual wanderings on the highlands and from its skin they made shoes and saddle-bags.

We are now in the borderlands of the high mountains. Swollen grey clouds rain lugubriously on a landscape which yesterday seemed so splendid under the sun's brilliance. The mountains weep, wrapped in a chill veil. But there are no yaks at Tukcha; they have still to come down from their pastures at Donkadsung and Samda, now beginning to be stricken by the first blizzards. The Moala pass is already blocked.

Tukcha would be a most pleasant place, were it not for the fury of an inexorable wind which rises about eleven o'clock every morning and rages until nightfall, repelled by the inflexibility of the rocks and made thereby even more spiteful and persistent. Stretched at ease with big houses along the banks of the Gandaki river, Tukcha is dominated by the Annapurna range on the one side and the peaks of Dhaulaghiri on the other; the snow has come down very low and has reached the sheltered slopes. Nepal, as a sub-tropical landscape, may be said to end a few miles before Tukcha. At Nancard-song the dense vegetation stops and even the pines, the last to survive, disappear and are replaced by a shaggy undergrowth which heralds the Tibetan landscape, bare as a desert but golden under the deep blue of the sky.

With the appearance of Lamaism there ends what I would term the rice-culture, which has spread upwards, generally speaking, from the south-east, and there begins the culture of barley, dominant in Tibet; two civilizations and two ways of life, that of the warm damp plain and that of the cold dry mountain.

Tibetan Buddhism begins just at this point, with its monasteries (*gompa*) and an occasional small chapel; at Tukcha, Hinduism, here practised by the Sher Chan family, exists alongside it. However, neither of the two religions is so intolerant as not to accept many beliefs of the primitive religion which preceded them.

Tukcha is the capital of the Takh district; the people speak a dialect akin to Tibetan, though they are all bilingual and use Napalese and Tibetan impartially.

The trade between Tibet and Nepal is centred on Tukcha. There are no shops; but inside the houses there are very rich storerooms. The Tibetans barter salt, sheep, hides, wool and horses for flour, rice and the main Indian manufactures which come here by way of Butwal, another mart on the southern Indian-Nepalese border. At Tukcha we were quite at home, under the vigilant protection of the Sher Chan family who are the real masters of this area. But my eagerness to leave gave me an aversion even for the house where the Sher

Chan family had installed me as their guest. It had no doors and enormous rooms through which the wind rushed whistling to the accompaniment of a baying of dogs which seemed to be lamenting their misery and their hunger. We even became bored by the invitations to lunch with which the worthy Sher Chan family oppressed us pitilessly. There were lunches at all hours of the day, even at eight in the morning, with curry, sharks' fins and noodles; it must have been their principal entertainment to watch us, as it was ours to eat, or pretend to eat, while they seated themselves opposite to study our every gesture and comment. We had nothing else to do and had come to the point when we considered it a great relief if there was a patient to visit. So all three of us went as a committee, Amorosino as the doctor, I to act as interpreter and Signorina Bonardi as nurse. The Tibetan doctor who had studied at Lhasa was still there to carry on his trade, looking better fed than ever, and since it seemed that he had been cured of tuberculosis by merit more of antibiotics than of prayer our remedies inspired more confidence than potions and incantations. The first tremor of changes that may lead it very far has begun to be felt in this country drowned in a sea of mountains. Inevitably, because, little by little, hearing of nearby places which are acquiring a new life, the people are becoming aware with dismay of how terribly backward they have remained and are trying to move quickly in order to make up for lost time. The wind of change may blow from either side, from the south or from the north. Tibet, over which China keeps close watch and ward, is only a few days march away.

Towards the Tibetan zones of Nepal

At dawn on the 5th we were ready. But to leave was a different matter. The yaks did not resign themselves to

renouncing their quiet pastures; they kicked, tossed the
cases from their backs and sent them crashing to the
ground. The caravan men yelled. One rushed to catch
a fugitive yak, another, left alone with an intractable
animal, used his teeth to help knot the cords and the
halter, while the local urchins sat around on the ground
watching, half naked in the fury of the wind. The sunlight slid over the frozen slopes of Annapurna. Everything went well as far as Marpa, but when we were half-
way through the village there was another catastrophe.
I was just holding my own against the wife of the abbot
of the monastery, who had rushed gleefully to meet me
and almost kissed me, and who wanted to drag me by
force to her husband's monastery when suddenly a yak
struck the corner of a case against the wall of a house, became frightened and began to run wild. The whole herd
went mad, jostling one another, pushing, butting, running, crashing their burdens against the walls, breaking
the cords and strewing the street with cases which burst
open at the impact. Tins, medicines, clothes, took wings
through the steep and narrow streets. The caravan men
rushed yelling after the beasts whilst we, amid the
laughter of the whole village, unhappily picked out of
the mud the scattered fragments of the havoc. God alone
knows when we shall arrive this evening.

The path skirts the Gandaki river as far as the bridge at
Jomosom where customs officials examine the merchan-
dise and collect the dues on caravans in transit. The
eastward path on the left bank of the river goes either
to Muktinath and Mana or to Mustang. The route to
Charka, however, goes westward and rises to Donkardsong (10,330 feet). Here there was another involuntary
halt; at the guard house Indian soldiers and Nepalese
officials were stationed to keep watch on the caravans
descending from the north. They came to meet us, shook

11. *The women of Charka return to their village
carrying loads of firewood.
In the foreground, stones
with engraved spells and prayers.*

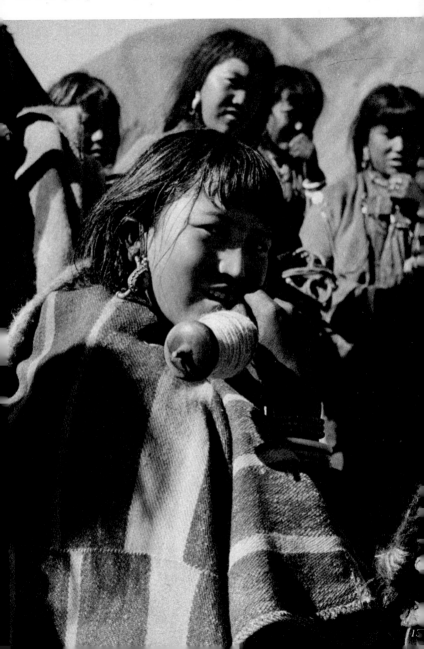

14

15. *Bonpo prayers carved on a stone at Tarap.*
    This custom is common to both Bonpo and Buddhists, but the words differ.
    The Buddhists walk around these low walls,
    keeping them always on their right; the Bonpo always keep them on their left.

16. *The Bonpo pantheon represented in fresco in a Bonpo temple.*
    Save for some iconographic details,
    many of the Bonpo deities are very similar to Buddhist ones.

hands with us and invited us to take tea with them. They thrust us into a large room which served them both as dormitory and kitchen. A Tibetan whom we had met at Tukcha in the earlier expedition of 1952 was making tea. A recent immigrant from Eastern Tibet he had now been engaged as interpreter, mainly to discover if under the robes of a pilgrim or a Tibetan merchant some Chinese agent might not be concealed. His new office and the unaccustomed salary had made him so happy that he could no longer control himself; he swilled *chang* from morning till night, but even at this hour he could no longer stand upright and the tea fell on our clothes instead of in the cups.

Even then the situation was changing rapidly and today it is even more changed. Along the track that descends from Mustang or the other that passes by Mana or that more easterly one starting from Chirong that crosses the Himalayas in the vicinity of Everest, the modest but continual traffic between India and Tibet has filtered for centuries. At the beginning of winter the merchants come down to sell horses and wool, and the pilgrims betake themselves, march by march, to visit the holy places of Buddhism, the dream of all Tibetans and the crowning moment of their lives. There were no passports; they came and went at will. Now all is changed.

The controls are very strict on both sides of the frontier; Indian soldiers to the south and Chinese soldiers to the north keep close watch. The Tibetans, by nature very independent and impatient of discipline as are people in whom the ancient flame of the nomad is not yet quenched and who wander without other restraints than those of the climate and the pastures on these immense highlands, are forsaking the customs of the caravans. These are dying out, with notable damage to the trade which is now channelled towards the new

C

roads that China has built throughout all Tibet to make effective her control over the country over which she claims ancient sovereignty.

We finally managed to take our leave just as the sun was going down; the track threaded a precipitous gully and then, wriggling between rocks and sliding through very high galleries, led us on to a plateau which looked to us endless. The twilight violet little by little faded out; the twinkling of the first stars heralded the night and we still went on plodding along that damned road. We arrived at Donkardsong when we could no longer see it a yard away and had to pitch our tents in the court of some squalid hovels among yaks, milch-cows and sheep: stink, baas and moos. An infernal night. But at dawn Annapurna in a splendour of light reminded us that things of beauty are always difficult to attain.

We were now in real Tibet though we had not crossed the frontier. The halt at Donkardsong was after all of some use. I got proof that in the end the unexpected change of itinerary imposed upon us by the season had turned to our advantage. The lama of the one little temple in the village assured me that in these parts the old Bon religion, which preceded Buddhism in Tibet and has now entirely disappeared save in the most distant provinces near China, still exists. According to him both Charka and Tarap were entirely Bonpo villages with temples and monasteries of that religion. Such reports have always a relative value, and more than once I have had cause to prove their lack of foundation; but this time a Bonpo manuscript that the lama showed me and finally, after long bargaining, sold me, gave me reason to hope.

The next day's march brought us to the foot of the Moala pass and we pitched camp at 12,000 feet. Facing us the huge massif of the Annapurna stretched out in an awesome saw-edge of glistening ice-fields over which broken cloud spread wisps of mist; to the north the valley of the Gandaki river vanished behind dishevelled ridges of absurd colours running in the direction of Mustang; straight in front of us Muktinath and the Mana pass were sleeping, bathed in the white silence of winter. Towards nightfall the sky lowered and it began to snow. The temperature went down below freezing point. Our fate was at the mercy of the caprices of the weather; a tempest may be unchained at the end of the season from one moment to the next, which would make it uncertain whether we would ever emerge from that icy beauty which beleaguered us. In places like this man returns to his origins; defenceless, humiliated by the caprices of nature which inspire in him only the supplication of despair. Nothing here resembles our friendly and welcoming lands, created solely for man to take possession of them, to till them, to tame them. Here nature is destruction, arrogance, an unchaining of primaeval violence; it is extravagant in everything, in creation and in destruction. Man is overwhelmed. Only religion aids him; it casts him head over heels, stripped of personality, into this rhythm of life and death, intoxicates him with its vehemence as he drags on his existence in this pitiless cycle of change. Then arise the Indian religions, of Shiva and of Durga. Or perhaps he himself will sublimate his own solitude in space into a metaphysical solitude, a void in which he and all things are eclipsed. And that will be Buddhism.

NEAR THE TIBETAN FRONTIERS

THE map is, as usual, inaccurate. There are huge empty spaces or approximate indications. Many names of rivers and mountains are wrongly spelt; I ask people where they are and they might as well have fallen from the clouds. No one has ever heard of them. What is true of the districts through which we are now passing is even more true in the north, where we shall have to skirt the confines between Tibet and Nepal, mere lines drawn on a terrain far from being exactly surveyed and demarcated. It is a border that the harshness of the landscape and the desolation and inaccessibility of nature has always seemed sufficient to defend. It runs through areas where there is very little life and where it is never possible to induce anyone to settle. There are, therefore, certain areas of Nepal, like Mustang, of Tibetan culture, where Lamaism has been penetrating for centuries and which even now, by ancient tradition, look towards Tibet, honouring the abbots of the famous Tibetan monasteries (mGor or Saskya in Central Tibet) and ruled by kings who boast their descent from the ancient Tibetan dynasties. These can become further causes—as we have seen quite recently—of serious conflict between China, which has absorbed Tibet, and India which, in her own interests, keeps watch over the frontiers of the neighbouring Himalayan state. No irreconcilable conflict could ever arise over such bleak uplands; disputes no less grave than those which have arisen over the

Sino-Burmese frontier have been settled to the satis-
faction of both sides. But less obvious causes may be
concealed behind a pretence of territorial claims. Then
matters become complicated and no one can predict how
they will end.

Over the high passes to Charka
The two passes which we must cross before reaching
Samda follow closely one after the other; the first, according to the caravan men, is called Dele (13,566 feet) and
the second Pemalochung (13,976 feet). The snow is deep
and we walk with difficulty through a luminous and
blinding silence along the trail traced out by the yaks.
We are in the midst of a frozen precinct enclosed by icy
walls; on the left, a few hundred yards from the track
the icefields rise in slow waves furrowed by mauve
powder-snow. By evening, we are at Samda-yarsa, 'the
summer settlement' (12,140 feet).

At Samda the first revolt took place. Departure was
fixed for seven. Everything was ready, the tents rolled
up, the cases placed two by two on the ground ready to
be hoisted on to the yaks; but nine o'clock came and not
even the ghost of a yak was to be seen. Only one of the
caravan men gave a sign of life, and that was to tell us
that the yaks were not to be found and that the other
men had gone to look for them. It was clear that he was
lying. The caravan men were all from Samda; they were
giving a helping hand to their own families intent on
turning the barley left to dry on the roofs of the terraced
houses, and had no wish to set out. We, however, could
not afford to lose even a day. I ordered the *sardar*, Lal
Singh, to go to the village at once and put an end to
these delays; but he was afraid and came back with his
tail between his legs, having accomplished nothing. So
I laid my plans with Pasang, who was more energetic;

if the caravan men should get the better of us, we would be at their mercy and slaves to their caprices. I knew by experience gained in my Tibetan expeditions that in such circumstances the only way to extricate oneself is by firmness. The leader of the caravan, whose unkempt hair and boorish manners made him look like a brigand, raised his voice at Pasang's remonstrances; but Pasang, who had taken the precaution of arming himself with a heavy cudgel, leapt on him like a flash, snatched the dagger which these men always carry with them, and boxed his ears soundly. The other, despite his truculent manner, fell on his knees, begged for mercy and went off at once to fetch the yaks. Before leaving Samda, I had all the daggers handed over to me. Because of this delay, we were forced to camp at sunset in the valley of the Remda river. We could see in front of us the huts of Samda-gunsa, 'the winter settlement', where the inhabitants of the village of Samda-yarsa will go for shelter in a few days time; it is situated higher up, but fully open to the south and sheltered from the winds.

The pass is a long way away and we had to climb from 12,140 to 17,552 feet; after crossing the Kibarla, 16,076 feet, which led us into a narrow upland valley surrounded on all sides by snow-clad mountains, we attacked, two hours later, the second pass which is known to the caravan men by the name of Barlagnika, 17,552 feet. The snow became deeper and deeper, the slope precipitous and slippery; some of the yaks almost fell and there was a tumult of cases crashing and caravan men yelling and the great black bodies seemed to tremble on the brink before righting themselves. Dusk began to fall and the snow to freeze. The yaks were almost exhausted, at the limit of their endurance, panting and halting every few minutes; in the end, about five o'clock, we reached the top of the divide, just in time to pitch camp on the level below before night overtook us. The camp was at 16,400 feet. My two companions were suffering slightly from mountain sickness, a natural result of weariness and cold. I was, however, surprised that the Tibetans too were overcome; Pasang and I were the only ones to remain well. The Tibetans, however, had been expecting this; at Tukcha they had warned us that this pass 'made the head spin'. Naturally they attributed this indisposition more to the influence of certain malign spirits than to the height. The next morning the caravan men were in sorry plight and the yaks, scattered in distant pastures, could not be found. Once more our departure was delayed. In any case it is not too easy for a yak-caravan to cover the distance between the pass and Charka in a single day; we trekked across plateaux that succeeded one another like an immense staircase, leaden and chill, till we reached the little valley (15,256 feet) where the caravans that pass this way usually spend the night. But there was no one there. The silence of the snowfalls was like a pause in the fury of the wind which flailed the air.

The temperature went down to more than twenty degrees below freezing point, but the caravan men almost always slept in the open. All around us the ice-fields bit into the expanse of deep blue sky which quickly turned ashen at the approach of sunset. We seemed transported into a planet devoid of life.

The Bonpo temples
Next day, having crossed the Tenge river, we reached Charka; a thin whitish twilight was slowly closing in as we arrived at the few houses that smoked on the savage hillside. The village is divided into two parts, one to the right and the other to the left of the river. On the left bank are the temples and a few dilapidated hovels; there

is no bridge and to go from one bank to the other one must ford the river, violent, swollen and icy. They had told us at Kathmandu and at Tukcha that the people of Charka were savages and they really seemed so both in their appearance and in their attitude towards outsiders; but little by little their shyness was dissipated. Astonished that I spoke their language and surprised to hear that I had been many times in Tibet, their reserve melted. They invited us into their houses and opened the doors of their chapels to us. The few temples on the left bank of the river were in bad repair and had been greatly damaged during the many wars between Tibet and Nepal, but they were enough to confirm the reports given me by the monk at Donkardsong. The religion professed by this village was that of Bon, organized into a system by Mi-bo-shen-rab, who was born in Western Tibet a few days march away, perhaps in the eighth century. Both Tarap and Charka thus boast of harbouring a priest who is a direct descendant of that illustrious master. But Bon today has been contaminated by its centuries of contact with Buddhism.

My investigations forced me to remain at Charka for two days. The yaks profited by this and wandered off to distant pastures; the men wasted a whole day looking for them and two could not be found. The people of Charka took refuge all day by the walls of their houses, on the sunny side where they were sheltered from the wind. There they wove the woollen blankets that the merchants from Tukcha or Jumla come to buy. They rested there in the sun, the men bare to the waist, the women with their cloaks open in front showing their breasts, while around them screeched and rolled their naked offspring. Life is reduced to barest essentials. Their endurance of this misery is tempered by the resistance given them by their religion which accepts resignedly the inevitable pains of existence. Which is better, their resignation without desires or the never satisfied and often cruel afflictions of progress?

From Charka there are two roads that we can take; the one southward follows the valley which the local people call Mulung and passes under the shadow of Dhaulagiri, finally ending at Tarakot. This was the road taken by Tichy in 1953. The other rises northwards, surmounts two passes and leads to Tarap which, according to the reports we had received, should be an important Bon centre. I therefore chose the northern route. When we left, the entire village was in a ferment; two or three players preceded us sounding the flutes used in religious ceremonies, the elders of the village escorted us and a noisy tail of women and children brought up the rear. I do not think that this was due to gratitude for the little good that we had been able to do them, healing some of their sick and paying generously for two or three of the blankets that they weave, or giving offerings to their private chapels. Gratitude does not come into it, since, in Buddhism and generally speaking also in Hinduism, gratitude, if it exists, should be felt by he who gives and not he who receives, since the latter has been the cause of a good action which, to the full advantage of the former, will inevitably by the iron law of Karma bring its own reward. The rejoicings that they made for us were the expression of a trustful friendliness. We had not been intruders come to sate our curiosity and then once more be engulfed in the indifferent void whence we had emerged. We had participated, were it only for a short time, in their life and on their own terms, made one with them in that common humanity within which, as when face to face with death, all men become equal.

Then came two more long cold marches. The track

begins to rise towards the north-west immediately after leaving Charka and reaches the pass of Sharginola (15,863 feet) near which we pitched our camp; on the slopes some Khampa nomads were driving herds of plump yaks. Here no frontier is marked and one has some idea of what might be the only liberty conceded to man. Liberty is possible only in such empty spaces; once put up a house, build a city or settle, and liberty becomes a word that everyone interprets in his own way in order to impose his will or his power.

Meetings on the uplands

On October 15th we tackled the second pass which the caravan men call Shargula (17,142 feet). All around us was a glistening crown of snow; we were on an island emerging from a sea of ice. A bitter wind was blowing which, finding no resistance, turned upon itself. The Himalaya was spread out before our eyes but, in order not to be seen, it concealed itself in a dazzling brilliance. A musket-shot away Dhaulagiri spread its pinions to the sky as if wishful to touch it and then fell earthward in horrible convulsions, recovered and dissolved into an immense whiteness of snow. On this pass also there was a pile of stones that the piety or fear of passers-by had raised. On the top varicoloured rags fluttered in the wind. On them were printed prayers and invocations. On every summit lives or hovers a spirit; it must needs be propitiated so that it may be friendly and not become offended by this violation of its dwelling-place. It is enough to throw a stone on the heap, murmuring the customary spell, in order to appease it.

The path did not slope but fell downwards towards Tarap through a most desolate landscape; the river that ran down the valley had overflowed into countless rivulets all frozen into ice. In such solitude any unexpected meeting with another person almost bewilders one; one does not know whether they be men or phantoms. We had two such meetings. A monk of the Red Sect wanted to come to our aid against the hostile powers that infest these inaccessible places. He sat down yogi-fashion, cross-legged, and began to recite, with slow modulations of his voice, the propitiatory charms. He accompanied the murmur of his prayers with the rhythm of a little drum and marked his pauses by whistling on a tiny trumpet made from a human shinbone. Under the Tarap pass another pilgrim joined us. Both came from the frontiers of China. One had been on his way for almost a year, the other for eight months, and both were heading for those places in India where Buddhism has left its eternal memories. To undertake such hard journeys alone, across such difficult and desert places and to support the extremes of the climate, there must be something more than physical vigour or force of will. It must be that the relation between man and nature is different from what it seems to us. Nature, for us, is the opposite of man, a balance of fixation and movement. These pilgrims see it through other eyes; it is the habitation of invisible presences who do not change their moods to suit man's whims. In itself, nature is inert; it cannot cause fear or represent any obstacle. The perils are not in it, but in the presences that rule it; it is therefore unnecessary to guard against the fickleness of the climate or the hardships of the road, or to provide oneself with means to overcome them. The solitudes are not deserted; they are, on the other hand, densely populated. Rites, suitable spells, exorcisms; these are the viaticum of the pilgrim. With such means he travels in safety. If these presences which he does not see but which he knows are near are favourable to him, then he has nothing to fear: rivers in spate, avalanches and landslides do not affect him.

When he is hungry he will find someone who will give him to eat. The endurance of these pilgrims lies wholly in their faith.

Goodbye to the yaks

Tarap (13,780 feet) is made up of several hamlets scattered along both banks of the river, six or seven in all. The barley has already been harvested and the yaks are busy ploughing the land for the next sowing. The people devote themselves mainly to stock-breeding since in such cold and high districts—the hamlets are all more than thirteen thousand feet up—only barley can grow (and that sickly and stunted). They trade with Tibet and the other provinces of Nepal. From Tibet they import rock-salt and sell it in the Nepalese markets, together with wool and the blankets woven by both men and women in their hours of leisure. As at Charka, one gets the impression that time and the current of history have forgotten this corner of the earth, forsaken amid the highest mountains in the world; it is like an unexpected leap into the past, a retracing of the passage of the centuries.

The soil is yellow in stony pallor; primitive nomadism has not retreated before sedentary life. The tiny fields of barley grow green for a few months but on the highlands the flocks and herds move endlessly, following the rhythm of the seasons. It is full moon, and the day of the full moon is feasted in Tibet. The two reasons, the religious and the profane, are superimposed; the rites are prescribed by religious tradition, but the people leave the more strictly liturgical portion to the lama, and adapt or modify them at will, inserting new themes.

Life in the open is coming to an end. The approach of winter changes the rhythm of life. Those who do not descend into the valleys with the flocks and herds shut themselves up in their houses to spin and weave. Some leave, others remain. There is both thanksgiving and farewell in their dances and songs, the promise of love and the sorrow of parting. The youth of the village range themselves in two files, facing one another and holding hands; on one side the men and on the other the girls. The men are the first to sing and draw closer to the women with tiny steps; when they have finished they retire very softly, while the girls reply in chorus. The songs, very sad, swell in monotonous modulations skyward under the cold light of the moon, like the wailing of earthbound creatures. They recall to me the voices of the jungle, laden one and all with a despairing pain. I have never listened to a more lacerating plaint than the cry of a tiger in the forests of Bengal; it has never terrified me, I do not know why, but always moved me to pity.

The people speak Tibetan and still follow the Bon, the primitive religion of Tibet prior to Buddhism which has little by little conquered the Country of the Snows. Over the crudity of its first shamanistic beliefs the Bon has little by little spread a mantle of greater dignity; ideas and ceremonies have been borrowed from Buddhism and very probably also from Manicheism and Nestorianism which found their way into Tibet along the Central Asian trade-routes which for centuries linked East and West. From these more advanced religions the followers of Bon accepted the idea that the world is a continual struggle between good and evil; good is a pure light that shines, uncontaminated, within us; we must defend it against the darkness of the shadows that threaten to quench it, and must struggle to restore it to its original freedom and clarity. The Bonpo do not, in the Tibetan manner, expose their dead in the mountains where the wolves and the vultures erase all traces in a very short time, nor do they burn them as do the Hindus—and

45

would not be able to do so since in this stony and pitiless desert not even a twig grows—but throw them into the rivers.

Along the wayside one comes across many *chorten*. This is the Tibetan name for certain monuments that correspond, though the form is often markedly different, to the Indian *stupa*. On a square base, sometimes made of superimposed steps, rises a sort of cupola topped by a number of round discs held together by a central axis which keeps them suspended. They may contain relics of saints or books or ritual objects no longer in use, and are therefore honoured as sacred. It is an action of the greatest merit to have one built and to take part in its construction, and it is a duty for the pious to walk around them, keeping them always on the right. But the Bonpo, although accepting the Buddhist form in its architectural plan and for similar aims, carry out the ritual encircling keeping the building always on their left. This is one of the principal formal differences between the two religions. One of the symbols of Buddhism is the swastika with its arms pointing to the right; that of the Bonpo is the same swastika pointing left. Otherwise the architecture of the Bonpo temple does not differ, in these districts, from that of the Buddhist; it is always a rectangular room, with or without a portico supported by wooden columns. On the wall at the back is the altar on which is placed the statue of the divinity to whom the chapel is consecrated; sometimes a covered corridor surrounds the edifice, which serves for the ritual perambulation. There are many of the small stone walls with engraved invocations and prayers which are so common in Tibet. But there is a great difference; whereas the Buddhist inscriptions contain almost always the formula of invocation to the god of mercy: *Om mani padme hum*, here the inscriptions are Bonpo.

It might seem impossible that in small communities like these, remote from all human contact, there should be room for more than one religion. But alongside the Bon there is also Buddhism, which has penetrated recently through the work of a few Tibetan ascetics. These can be recognized at sight by the long tresses coiled around their heads in the manner of a turban. These are artificial tresses, bought or donated to increase the distinction of the person and as a visible sign of the ascetic virtues attained. Such ascetics are experts in the magic arts, therefore their services are in demand to heal the sick, drive away epidemics or dispel the evil forces that wait everywhere in ambush to menace the lives and fortunes of men. Always on the march from village to village, never stopping at a monastery, they sleep in the open, even in these exceedingly cold districts; every so often they disappear and seek refuge in the depths of some cave far distant from the well-trodden tracks in order to give themselves up, undisturbed, to their spiritual exercises, sure of maintaining intact in this way their thaumaturgic abilities. There is no doubt that with practice they acquire strange and unusual powers; they succeed in controlling their own thinking and are able to produce in themselves a voluntary control of their body temperature, which they call *tummo*, by virtue of which they engender such heat in their bodies that they are able to remain for a considerable time stark naked under the fury of the terrible Himalayan winds, and to work other wonders due mainly to breath-control and suggestion.

At Tarap a white-robed long-haired priest claimed direct descent from the teacher Bon who was born not far away and of whom I have already spoken, and who conferred the dignity of dogma on the primitive shamanistic beliefs. Crouched in the half-light of the temple he recited interminable liturgies in a monotonous voice, beating the shamanistic drum in cadence and swaying to the drumbeats; on the altars slumbered incomprehensible images in which rejoice and are extolled the presages and complexities of one of the least known religions in the world.

The countryside is bleak but rich; rich because the inhabitants are nearly all merchants who trade with Upper Nepal and Tibet.

Here too the women, as is the case throughout Tibet itself, have great authority. The village of Tarap is in fact ruled by a woman, whom we called the 'mayoress'. She was middle-aged and vigorous in manner and ways of speech; everyone had a great respect for, and perhaps fear of, her. In contrast to the Tibetans the women of these parts do not go in for the luxury of those broad strips of wool hanging down from the head and covered with turquoises, corals and silver coins, like the nomads of Western Tibet who prefer to carry their treasures on their own persons rather than entrust them to others. Also the earrings are not remarkable and often are not worn at all. The sole ornament in which these women take pride is a curious strip of beaten silver with rolled-up edges, sometimes inset with turquoises, which they wear bound to the nape of the neck.

Many roads converge on Tarap. One to the north-east leads to the monastery of Panjar and thence by an easy pass to Tibet; another, branching from the road to Pale, climbs to a high pass and joins the Jumla and Rimi road; it has the great advantage of being practicable for yaks. However the sky, which had begun to cloud over, dissuaded me from following the shortest route, and the people of Tarap also foretold a change in the weather and insisted that I take no risks in so advanced a season in a difficult area and on a road which

20. *The Tibetan owner of the yaks of our caravan.*

21. *Our camp on the slopes of Annapurna.*

22. *Tibetan pilgrims seated on a rock watch our caravan as it ascends the Shargula (17,150 feet).*

23. *Lal Singh shelters from the wind on the Barlagnika Pass (17,570 feet).*
On the top of every pass (la rtse) *there stands a small structure or pile of stones known as* Lha t'o, *'the house of the god' who lives on the mountain.*
Every passer-by adds a stone to the pile, reciting the charm lha rgyal lo *(pronounced la jallò),*
'the god has conquered'.

24, 25. *Typical caravaneers.*

26 (overleaf). *After a rest, the caravan
is once more ready to go on its way.*

27. *Bells, flowers and cloths*
  appease the spirits that haunt the wayside.

28, 29. On the road between Pale and Jumla images of gods protect fields and homes; though not funerary in character, they remind one of the tomb-figures of Kafiristan.

30 (overleaf). A wayside shrine dedicated to a bhut, a local spirit, with images of donors. The architectural influence of the Buddhist stupa is evident here.

crosses two passes both more than fifteen thousand feet high. There remained only the path which, skirting the Tarap river and fording it no less than seventeen times, joins the valley of the Bheriganga below Pale. Moreover, in districts so sparsely populated a rather large caravan, such as mine, cannot be assembled in a moment. We are not in Tibet where every person permitted to enter that forbidden land is provided with a *laissez-passer* by virtue of which the local authorities are obliged to procure means of transport according to the government tariff and provide the means of support that the countryside affords. In Nepal the only reason that induces the people to enrol is poverty. When great caravans are not organized at Kathmandu for the duration of an expedition returning to the same spot, as is the case with the greater number of those intended for the conquest of some Himalayan peak, there are difficulties at every stage, either owing to the scarcity of the population or because wherever there is a chance to make money the porters try to exploit this opportunity to the full; or perhaps the men are kept back by their labours in the fields or delayed by festivals such as the Dussera, which falls in October.

In 1952 I broke up the first caravan at Tukcha because it was unable to continue the journey in the cold climate of Mustang and Muktinath; another accompanied me from Muktinath to Butwal and a third from Bhutval to Pokhara.

This year the changes were even more frequent; the first caravan was from Pokhara to Tukcha, a second, with yaks, from Tukcha to Tarap, a third from Tarap to Pale, a fourth from Pale to Tibrikot, a fifth from Tibricot to Jumla, a sixth from Jumla to Dullu, a seventh from Dullu to Surkhet, and an eighth from Surkhet to Nishangara. But I always took the precaution of sending ahead either Lal Singh or someone else to announce my imminent arrival and make advance arrangements for the hiring of men and to agree on prices and conditions. Moreover, despite the authoritative letters of the Minister of Foreign Affairs and the Commander-in-Chief, I was often compelled to postpone my departure longer than intended. Considerable difficulties also arose about rates and methods of payment. I do not know how affairs stand now, but during the journey which I am describing Nepalese money was no longer current as soon as one had left Pokhara, and even where it was in use its value varied; the new issue did not circulate except in Kathmandu and places nearby. From Pokhara onward the porters refused to accept it and only the old silver coins and Indian rupees were in circulation. At Jumla, and from Jumla down to the Terai, only Indian money was accepted.

At Tarap we left the yaks. We took four days to reach Pale. The road was a dangerous one. A noisy column of porters, women for the most part, leaped from rock to rock like a herd of ibex; the younger girls, slender and talkative, outdid the men in resistance. A fringe of hair fell coquettishly over their foreheads, but the toil and the harsh weather soon mark their agreeable faces with the wrinkles of an early old age. In the evenings they camped in the open in the shelter of some cave or warmed themselves around the great campfires which sketched remarkable moving pictures in the shadows.

Men and women sang antiphonally till overcome by sleep. Then they fell asleep, one upon the other, in the icy breath of the night.

THE DISCOVERY OF THE MALLA

AFTER four days of very hard march we descended to the Bheriganga. Bamboos were growing sheltered by the firs, but we were still nine thousand feet up. Here Tibetan culture ends like a wave that dies upon the sand. It begins to get too warm for the mountaineers. As we go onward we pass from one ethnic group to another, as if the rivers and the mountains had enclosed the various tribes in oubliettes, chaining them to the soil.

Pale is the last village where the Bonpo religion still survives and where Tibetan is spoken; a few miles away Hinduism begins, with an occasional sporadic Buddhist survival still evident in a few poor chapels and in the *chorten* which, ever more infrequent, shine white along the wayside.

Hinduism has penetrated slowly from India, has prospered and has made itself at home. But it has been a superficial conquest only, in the sense that while it has assimilated native beliefs and given its own names to local cults, it has in fact adapted itself to a primitive religious world wherein the terror of men faithful to the cruel motherhood of the earth holds sway. The cabins which serve as temples remind one strangely of the holy places of Polynesia; in their interiors rough-hewn stones reveal the dread presence of the deities and depict the inevitable cycle of life and death while around them swarm the wooden images of ancestors.

The rule of Hinduism begins again

At Tibrikot, on the crest of a spur, the temple of Tripuransudari tinged with red and fearsomely grim overlooks the valley. The name is Indian, but the goddess worshipped under this name does not have the precision of outline of the Indian goddess; she is an obscure force of nature, capriciously generous and cruel. In the forecourt a Pale painter who, as a caravan man, had accompanied me as far as the village, has painted one alongside the other the deities of Hinduism, of Buddhism and even of the Bon religion. Three religions, represented by the symbols of their gods or leaders, live together in close brotherhood in the same temple.

The goddess has not yet revealed her terrible divinity in an image but is imprisoned in a stone. So it is everywhere in this valley, where temples are rare and often do not exist at all. Stones are placed at the foot of a tree, both they and the tree sharing an obscure sense of the divine. The tremendous force explodes in a thousand apparitions which have neither outline nor form but all, under different names, signifying, in fear and amazement, the same feeling of the wonder of life and of its continual renewal across the necessity of death. This feeling has had its highest philosophical and literary expression in India which has given the name of Kali to this rhythm of birth and death. 'Ever you dance, nude warrior, on the body of Shiva. The heads of your sons, daily cut off, form your necklace; the stumps of human arms hang from your girdle. Your face dazzles like the flower of the lotus and yet is terrible with its sempiternal smile. The hue of your limbs is like a stormcloud and your feet are flecked with blood.'

The same idea is expressed in a crude stele erected in a field near the roadway a little before Rimi. Here an expression has been given to this obscure force; it is no longer a presence which, even though omnipotent, no human eye sees, but a being that has assumed a form. Whoever carved the face on the great stele was certainly no artist, so childish is the technique and so out of proportion the drawing; none the less it does not fail to show effectively the dreadful nature of the being represented and the terror it inspires. The shrunken legs beneath the immense body accentuate the monstrousness of the image and give greater emphasis to the horrible head from which rises bristling, perhaps flaming hair. Notwithstanding its primitiveness, the figure holds its own in comparison with the more elaborate ones in India dedicated to Kali which succeed in expressing, as perhaps no other art does, the terror of man brought face to face with the mystery of life and death.

In some villages huge wooden stakes surmounted by hideous heads are set up before the houses as a protection. A trident is often placed on the head and the crude images bare their teeth in evil presage. This incubus weighs in the air, one breathes it in everywhere, it never leaves one and almost makes one forget the splendour of the sun in the clear autumn skies.

Thus there still exist in the heart of the Himalayas the religious complexities of India, though it were better to say they exist in an elementary form; the same awe of the divine presence and the same certainty that is revealed to man in all its myriad facets. In the places through which we are now passing we find this religious world in all its initial fervour and fury, without dogmatic outlines, in an extraordinary spontaneity that takes us back to the origins of the world. We are in a country where life is old, yet nothing has been changed, where man preserves immutably the phantasies and terrors, the imaginings and the hopes that in other

53

places the onrush of the centuries has transfigured or consigned to oblivion.

Once past Tibrikot, villages are few and seem like patches of brighter green inset among the firs and pines. A mosaic of races, one interlocked with another, has wound its way into these valleys and attempted to scale these mountains; massive and muscular Magars, slender Brahmans and those taciturn warriors the Khets.

The people always maintain a certain reserve. Weary of tinned food, we tried unsuccessfully to buy eggs and chickens of which there was an abundance. The refusal was courteous but irrevocable. Because of this suspicious reserve, the Aryan migrations which have for centuries penetrated into the heart of the Himalayas have tried to avoid mixed marriages and miscegenation; shipwrecked in a sea of diverse races they have wanted to keep themselves uncontaminated.

The grey and stormy curtain of cloud which for some days past had submerged the mountain chains justified my anxiety, never communicated to my travelling companions, to get out of the highlands as soon as possible before the change of the season closed the passes.

By great good fortune we managed to wriggle out just at the right moment, slipping out during the brief interval of good weather that shines on the Himalayan peaks at the close of the rainy season. The marches were made longer; the porters were tired and they filed along bent under their burdens through the narrow valleys above which, on the summits, the splendour of the ice-fields floated in the sky.

These peoples, doubtless very ancient, appear as if they had only just emerged from a primaeval simplicity. The regime that governs them is a sort of village commune, an autonomous unit ruled by a council of five elders who elect their own head and have practically no contact with the central authority. In this country, without roads and without posts, without telephonic or telegraphic communications, without doctors or medicines, these little inhabited islands go on governing themselves. From these frontier areas which, because of the geographical conditions and the present circumstances, are in a very tense situation no news, even the most serious, can reach the capital in less than a month and then only by means of couriers exposed to the risks and perils of the paths and the climate. The government is a remote entity of which they talk only to stress its absence. What may have been done today to remedy this I do not know.

Throughout the five hundred miles of our journey we did not find I will not say a hospital but not even a dispensary or a nurse. At every halt the sick crowded around our camp seeking aid or comfort. Doctor Amorosino worked wonders in cures and medicaments, but for the more serious cases, and these were the majority, there remained only regret at not being able to do anything to save a life. The sick man bows to fate or relies on his own resources and endurance in the expectation that his destiny will be accomplished; this renunciation favours the resignation that controls his actions and sometimes seems a supreme indifference, as if the natural instinct of self-preservation, which we share also with the beasts, were extinguished among these peoples.

Jumla: the first inscriptions

The desolate magnificence of the provinces bordering on Tibet is by now far away; now we are launched into the forested labyrinth of the narrow Nepalese valleys. Every trace of cultivation disappears. Nature unrestrained by the counterpoise of the climate proliferates in intoxi-

cated exultation. Man himself is a part of nature. A be-
wildered immobility holds one in an inertia without
past; one moves in a virgin land. The sudden appearance of the first temple a little before Jumla, solitary in
a grass-grown hollow, is the unexpected sign that we are
about to emerge from this mute savagery. Stones worked
by man suddenly give a meaning to the landscape. After
the nothingness of nature absolute, where man can only
wonder or tremble, the prodigious breath of human
creation rises from these ruins. Contemplation of the
landscape is succeeded by the reawakening of the
imagination striving to gather and integrate the ancient
voices suspended in these works.

After seven days of uninterrupted march, crossing
two passes, one of 12,250 feet and one of 12,500 feet,
we arrive at Jumla. We are now at our thirty-second
camp. The valley widens; the river, as if tired of
its precipitous rush through the rocks, rests in the
shelter of wide banks along which lies the chessboard of
the ricefields; a necklace of little villages suns itself
against a background of rectangular straw-ricks that
from a distance one might take for the walls of ancient
fortresses. Herds of horses, which recall the cavalry
which at one time conquered western Tibet and for
three centuries held it in subjection, graze on the grassy
hills and form, together with the rice, the main wealth
of the country. No longer needed for war, they are bred
for peaceful trade.

We had hoped to find at Jumla the field-radio that
should have been able to link the town with Kathmandu
and thus be able to communicate through my friends in
the Nepalese capital with the rest of the world. But it
was a hope soon dashed; the apparatus was there to be
sure but, as I had suspected, it was not working.

In compensation our forecast about the historical im-

32 (overleaf). *A huge* stupa *built on the model of Svaymbhunath, the most famous Buddhist sanctuary in Nepal.*

33

36. *A* stupa *at Donkardzung.*

38, 39. *Women of Tarap.*

40 (previous page). *A mustard-seed press at Dullu.*

41

41. 42, *Women of the Terai.*

43. *An Indian ascetic who has retired to the depths of the jungle to meditate.*

portance of Jumla was confirmed. The dynasties that had their seat there have left their traces in the stone temples, some Hindu, some Buddhist, now for the most part abandoned, and in the inscriptions. The evidence of this history appeared before our eyes in our daily walks. Kings until now unknown sang to us from the stones in the Sanskrit tongue the glories of their ancestors and their own deeds. Our enthusiasm fired the local authorities who, up to our arrival indifferent or ignorant, now suddenly felt themselves filled with unexpected archaeological ardour and fell over themselves to lend a hand. The official who was deputizing for the absent governor unleashed his personal bodyguard, for once stirred out of their customary ease, to search in villages and houses for family chronicles or royal donations inscribed on copper tablets sometimes gilded.

One thing is sure; Jumla today is a village that owes its well-being to its extensive and well-watered valley; but there is no doubt that it could support many more people. That was in fact the case in ancient times, when its kings had relations with Tibet and its craftsmen were so renowned as to be summoned to the Country of the Snows to cast there the images of the gods. From the names found in the first inscriptions and from the manuscripts we could deduce that this dynasty was the same as that called by the Tibetan historians sMal, that is to say the Malla. But, as our later discoveries at Dullu were to prove to us, this was not a question of a dynasty descended from the kings of Tibet, but rather one that had ascended from these parts and the nearby Garhwal for the conquest of that country.

We pushed on from Jumla to Dullu in a week. The porters scattered regardless of everything, torn away in haste, sometimes almost with violence, for the last labours in the fields before the cold, which already hung impatient in the air, should strangle every living thing upon the earth.

The second revolt took place. The march had really been a very long one, from dawn until nightfall. But there was no alternative, for we had found no trace of water save for that stagnating in the putrid and muddy ricefields. The first porters to arrive were exhausted. As soon as the tents had been pitched the last group of stragglers came in dead beat, grumbling and with malevolent expressions. Immediately they put down the cases they began to threaten Lal Singh and Pasang. Lal Singh trembled with fear; Pasang gripped his cudgel and courageously faced up to the most violent of them. When I saw that they were striking him and that the others were getting angry, I intervened. My presence quietened them and the tumult died down. In a few moments all was over. Like good-natured children, once the tantrums were over, they made peace with Pasang and grouped together around the campfires under a cloudy lowering sky. For that day they received double pay.

A poor man who had accompanied me like a shadow for the whole march held in his hand a copper cup filled with honey. He coughed every moment with a persistency that irritated me. As soon as we arrived he offered me the honey, and asked for the doctor to visit him. I do not know what was wrong with him, certainly something very serious. We offered to leave him some injections which might have helped him but he refused them with a disconsolate air, since in all that area there was no one who knew how to give them to him. He turned away with head hung low.

Dullu; the genealogy of the Malla
Dullu is a tiny state in the centre of Nepal. Its king,

who also boasts of his descent from the ancient nobility of India, has now become life-governor, but is subject to the ups and downs of politics and is more than a little afraid of them; with the advent of democracy he lost his kingdom for a year but, by the aid of friends in high places who had remained on top in the troubled sea of human fortunes, he got it back again in the end —for how long I would not like to say. Of his regal pomp all that remains today is his helmet from whose vizor hang, like a fringe, six large emeralds.

The armed forces and the police consist of eight men, and the seat of royalty is a small two-storey house in which, at sunset, there are not even oil-lamps. Isolated in such squalid solitude, he seeks to relieve the tedium with the garrulous company of three wives, the eldest of whom takes the cows to pasture from dawn till dusk. But even though his royal prerogative had fallen to so lamentable an estate, his hospitality was cordial. His Highness took much interest in my researches and presented me with a copy of his family chronicles and other documents preserved in his private archives.

At Dullu we were in a terrain of great archaeological importance which, by a stroke of good fortune, I was the first to explore. Long inscriptions on very tall steles contained the genealogy of the Malla kings and the record of their conquests. A colossal cistern built with cyclopean stone blocks records, in the inscription which runs right round it, the generous donations of a king and his ministers. What until yesterday was this part of Nepal? A geographical mystery, a disorder of valleys and mountains, where a people whose existence of disappearance left us totally indifferent struggled against isolation, climate and poverty.

Whereas elsewhere ruins are brought to life by the presence of man, this is a special land where it is the ruins and the evidence of the past which serve to bring the present to life. These villages which seem to be without history become once more a part of a tradition whose memory has been resurrected by our discoveries. Now they are returning to life; for the life of a people is founded on the dead and their resurrection. An empire was reborn before our eyes, the names of a few of whose kings had alone been preserved in the Tibetan chronicles. Yet for three centuries, from the eleventh to the fourteenth, they had governed a territory larger than Italy. It was not a brief chapter that the discoveries disclosed; complex events once again saw the light of day: bold and warlike men, driven out or alarmed by invasions or political upheavals, made their way across the Himalayan precipices, surmounted their crests and then descended into Western Tibet, conquering it and founding there a feudal empire, investing the ancient aristocracy with new privileges or creating from it a new one. Thus it reached the summit of its power but then, like all empires, due to too great an expansion or poor cohesion, internal revolts or the pressure of fresh inroads, it declined and fell, leaving in its place ephemeral lordships consumed by rival jealousies and conflicts, whose voices, ever more feeble, we can still hear almost to the beginning of last century. Indeed, with the inscriptions, we found also some chronicles in the Pahari language in which from time to time some notes of poetry still sounded.

On the whole, however, these documents were the usual miscellany of genealogies, arid lists of names suspended in the void of chronological uncertainty, glimpses of mythology and echoes of old Indian tradition.

The rivalry between two brothers, Mukti Sahi and Javani Bhan, inspires the beginnings of an epic; but the account does not succeed in rising above the banal and is quickly submerged in the conventionality of the usual legends; the uprightness of Javani, whom Mukti Sahi tries in vain to kill, and his countless adventures, struggles against serpents and lions, and warlike exploits from which the hero always emerges unscathed. But none the less the succeeding period of Prithivi Malla, perhaps the last of his dynasty, also begins to clear. Semja, north of Jumla, remained for some time the capital, but Western Tibet regained its independence, soon however to pass under the power of the kings of Ladakh until Tibet took final possession of it.

After the Malla kings lost their power, branches of the family continued to survive in obscurity, but a new historical situation was created whose central figures were Ganesvara and Baliraj, under whom Jumla became separated from Semja.

The progressive breaking-up of western Nepal into dozens of petty princedoms was hastened by the poverty of their resources and the restricted size of their territories, so that they declined more and more. Shut up within their narrow boundaries, cut off from their trade with India and Tibet and overwhelmed by the expansion of the less civilized tribes which thronged about them on all sides, they little by little stagnated in a cultural decadence in which even the memory of their former prestige was forgotten.

This is not the place to give the long list of names of the kings of the two dynasties, Pala and Malla; in all there are thirty-four of them. We even know the names of the wives of some of them. For almost two centuries the chronology is very clear, but it becomes confused in the succeeding period not only because the family chronicles, unsupported by contemporary documents or inscriptions, become uncertain but above all because of the proliferation of petty princedoms in which the events are interlocked and intertwined. But we now have in our hands the necessary facts to relate with greater accuracy the secular events of these regions, where seemingly contradictory happenings were contemporaneous or successive.

Let us go even farther into particulars; the genealogies engraved on the Dullu steles begin with the first adventurer—he was called Nagadeva—who in the twelfth century replaced the princes descended from the line of the ancient kings of Lhasa which was established in western Tibet; then they run from father to son down to the last, Prithivi Malla (fourteenth century) under whom the Malla Empire reached the height of its power, only to break suddenly into pieces and disappear. One of the first kings, who bore the glorious name of Asoka, even made a donation to Bodhgaya, the famous spot where the Buddha attained supreme enlightenment. We know this from an inscription which bears his name. Of course this was not merely an act of devotion but also a proof of munificence and power.

The steles found at Dullu and in the nearby villages are about six feet high and of dark stone. Incrustation and the long action of time have often damaged the letters. The writing is that in common use in these parts between the twelfth and fourteenth century. At the top is a Buddhist symbol, one of those *stupas* or *chorten* of which I have spoken; below, in the same characters which were used both in Tibet and Nepal to write the same formula, can be read the famous invocation to Avalokiteshvara: *Om mani padme hum*. The inscription also bears the name of the scribe who composed it, who sometimes attempts brief outbursts of verse inspired by conventional Indian themes. It can be seen that the links with Indian culture were slight, but what

62

is interesting is precisely that connection and cohabitation of Hindu cultural tradition and Buddhist symbols on the same stele. But in the course of our journey we came across many examples of this in other steles and in the presence, along the wayside, of *chorten* which have, however, a style of their own, half based on the architectural motives of the Indian temples and half resembling those of Tibet. Thus at Michigaon we found a whole forest of them, some of them inscribed, but dating from a later period. These were, however, of great interest not only because of their number, as dense as a stone forest, or because they showed the tenacity of Buddhism in a district more and more dominated by Hinduism, but mainly because we had the impression of taking part in the disintegration of an architectural form which, initiated in India in the times of the great Emperor Asoka, was to die out among these distant and degenerate Himalayan dependencies.

These unexpected discoveries gave us a lot to do since in some of the *chorten* the inscription ran around the base half buried in the earth. We had therefore to use every sort of flattery to overcome the reserve of the people who are always frightened and mistrustful when it is a question of excavating in places which they consider sacred. I succeeded in persuading them after generous gifts and more so when, to their surprise, they were compelled to realize that these letters which not even their priest knew how to elucidate were quite easy for me to decipher and understand. However, an old sorceress whom everyone held in great respect began to croak at the top of her voice about the sacrilege and we were forced to stop. By great good fortune she came on the scene when most of the work had already been done. In any case precise dates now shone like stars in the night of history and other inscriptions celebrated the new

63

capital built on the farther side of the Himalayas and revealed the brotherhood of the two religions, Buddhism and Hinduism, while names of ministers and poets and records of the munificence and donations of kings were registered with the essential aridity of legal documents.

Two families were revealed, the Pala and the Malla, later fused into a single stock by the extinction of the former; they were the boldest. With a first push forward, they made their way up the valleys of the Karnali and the other rivers and took possession of them. Then they spread out and extended their conquests, probably attracted by the goldmines of Tok-jalung and the rich wool- and salt-markets of western Tibet. After their conquest of this region, they became assimilated to the extent of taking Tibetan names, but none the less they did not abandon their old ones and enjoyed a two-fold nomenclature which indicated the twofold composition of their empire, twofold also from the religious viewpoint since, perhaps by tradition worshippers of Shiva, they became Buddhists in Tibet where the echo of the Buddhist apostolate of the twelfth century was still alive and where their predecessors, now reduced to a state of vassalage, had built the wonderful temples of Tsaparang and Toling which I had the good fortune to discover, and describe, in my voyages in 1931, '32 and '33. (North of the Himalayas they used Tibetan in their documents; and in the south Sanskrit.)

It was a kingdom of feudal type, since the newcomers did not drive out the local princes but forced them to recognize their suzerainty, leaving them free to retain their own institutions and their own beliefs.

The power and intelligence of the Malla kings is shown even today by their roads. As soon as we entered what might be considered the central core of their very extensive empire the narrow and dangerous paths,

44 (previous page). *An Indian ascetic rests in the shade, by the shrine of Shiva at Jumla.*

45. *Kanphat ascetic ('those of the pierced ears') by the shrine of Shiva at Jumla.*

46 (overleaf). *Shrine of the Malla period at Jumla.*

45

46

47, 48. Local and nameless gods stand guard over the fields to assure the fertility of the soil.

47

48

49. *Memorial inscriptions found by the wayside.*

50. *The discovery of inscriptions on the* stupas *of Michagaon.*

51. *Girls of Jumla.*

52. *Old women sit at home and spin wool for blankets or clothes to be sold in Kathmandu.*

53. *Harvesting barley at Jumla.*

54 A Newari peasant

carved out by the caravans for centuries without man having ever done anything to improve them, were replaced by wide roads. It was no longer nature alone which formed them; human hands had hewn them from the rocks, had built bridges and tried to protect them from landslides. The empire had been destroyed but the people still called this road *raja marga*, 'the royal road'. Every so often, on the stone blocks flanking it, inscriptions half erased by time, bore the name of the king and Buddhist invocations with the pious wish that the benefit of the completed work might be devoted to the spiritual profit of mankind. This road was therefore a confirmation of the wise state organization of the Malla. Without this road that bound together the extreme confines of their empire, composed of a human medley of varying tradition, language and customs, in part subjected but in part perhaps still eager to regain their lost liberty, they would not have been able to assure internal security or have been able to move troops easily from one part of their empire to another. It also served, in a much lesser degree, to further the trade that must have been one of the principal sources of their prosperity.

In their chronicles and monuments we can see clearly depicted their contacts with China and the reasons for their greatness and their final dismemberment. Other invasions from India soon followed.

The road from Jumla to Dullu is the route of those fresh warlike migrations which left India to find some recompense for their lost splendours in the unhealthy valleys of the Himalayas. The wanderings which led them here after the downfall of the Malla began (according to a tradition of which we hear the echo in the chronicles) immediately after the fall of Chitor, the solitary bulwark put up by Hindu resistance to the Moslem advance. Three times Chitor fell and twice rose again from its ruins. Always, when uncertain hope became the certainty of despair, of humiliation and of death, the women—and there were thousands of them—cast themselves on the pyre that they themselves had prepared, and the men, from the greybeards to the youths, in festal attire, flung open the gates and threw themselves on their assailants to break their way through or to die.

Many have doubted that the pretensions of the Nepalese nobility to be descended from the Rajput heroes might only be wishful thinking to increase their own prestige. The discoveries we had just made seem to show that there is some truth in the legend.

The path of these bands desperately intent on remaking a country for themselves can be traced on the stone steles set up in the places where these warriors died fighting; on the front, in a square frame, is the figure of an armed man holding his horse's reins. They are the same steles that light like stars the vast obscurities of many parts of India with the anonymous record of their sacrifice. But on these paths other monuments, of Buddhist inspiration, commemorate the heroism of the defenders in the brotherhood of death, unmindful, beyond the thresholds of eternity, of the hatred of the survivors.

We can also trace migrations of primitive tribes, heirs of the megalithic culture. What are those monstrous wooden images set up in the fields and near the houses in the valley of Rimi save survivals of megalithic cultures; and what are the stone steles erected along the roads of which I have spoken and which remind us of the pillars of the Naga peoples on the farthest confines of Assam, as if to record this swarming of the peoples who crisscross, clamber over one another and replace on another in these sub-Himalayan foothills, save the wake of migrations coming from the East? I willingly grant that many links are missing, but the fact remains that these discoveries throw light on many centuries, from primitive times when the dawn of history had not yet broken over the sub-Himalayan jungles down to the times of the rise and ephemeral flourishing of an empire upon which these ruins comment, and confirm the language of the documents.

The austere and simple solidity of the stone temples in the midst of the passive misery of the mud and straw hovels marks the borders of greatness and decline. Their number is a testimony to the downfall of a civilization, as if in the collapse everything had been enveloped in a dense mist or had been shattered into dust. The temples in their useless and empty loneliness seem to repeat the warning of the Indian poet that the substance of this world is death:

'Behold, in a house where there were once many, there has remained one only; and where there was one and then many, there remains in the end not one. Thus day and night, Shiva and Kali, move like pieces on the chess-board of the world, playing with human pawns."

These temples are not very large but they are beautifully built of stones accurately cut. The main part is made up of an open chapel, in the centre of which is the image or the symbol of the god. Over the chapel rises the pyramidal roof surmounted by a stone disc which the Indians call *amalaka*. In some cases there is a little porch in front of the chapel consisting of a stone which forms a roof supported by two pillars. Almost all the temples repeat a similar plan which, however, is not limited to these parts but is traceable to Indian tradition and to the surviving temples of neighbouring regions. The almost total absence of statues or other pictorial features save for some flowered ornaments which embellish the portals of certain temples is to be regretted. Dullu yielded only a fragment representing a Buddhist divinity, which shows a close stylistic connection with the early plastic works of Nepal and is descended from classical Gupta models (fourth-sixth centuries A.D.) A carved lion, half buried in the earth, had no grace and was devoid of any artistic value. This absence of works of art leads one to think of a war, a violent destruction in which the element of religious odium was not lacking. This must have taken place very shortly after the times of Prithivi Malla which marked the zenith of the power of the Malla but were none the less the end of the dynasty. After his time, as I have said, came the ruin caused by fresh migrations from India which led to the foundation of dynasties of more intolerant religious principles.

Origin, expansion and downfall of the Malla

Whence came these Malla kings, all of whose names we know from the first to the last? We cannot say with absolute certainty; it cannot however be denied that they belonged to the Khasia people, diffused throughout Kashmir and the nearby mountains as far as Simla and Gahrwal, and who are frequently mentioned in Indian literature. But the empire of Nepal and western Tibet was the most extensive kingdom that they succeeded in founding. The Malla had two capitals, the first at Taklakot on the far side of the Himalayas where ruins of great castles still exist. Today Taklakot is a little village which I have visited twice in the course of my Himalayan journeys.

They settled there probably immediately after the conquest, replacing the ancient kings of Tibetan origin, whom they made vassals. But Taklakot is a very cold place with few resources; furthermore the vicinity of unruly tribes soon forced the Malla to found a new capital, the winter capital, south of the Himalayas in the heart of Nepal where the climate is milder. This new capital was called Semja; the village still exists north of Jumla, but of its past only ruins remain. Certainly we cannot get an exact idea of its size or its magnificence from the praises celebrated in a diploma engraved on a bronze tablet in which Prithivi Malla grants special privileges to a family. The style of this inscription, written in Sanskrit filled with literary allusions and word-play and closely copied from the traditional themes of Indian poetry, does not allow us to take it too literally. But there seems to be no doubt that the city flourished, especially since it is situated in the centre of the caravan routes between the two parts of the Malla empire which, because of the goldmines around Kailasa and Tok-jalung, had accumulated so much wealth that it was often able to donate to the principal temples of Lhasa huge quantities of gold intended to regild their cupolas. It would be interesting to excavate in this part of the country in the hope that other evidence might still come to light.

Two completely different worlds co-exist here; on the one hand the present-day world, primitive and poverty-stricken, without material wealth and lacking that ardour of faith that throws the bridge of artistic creation between the present and the past; on the other the ancient world darkly immersed in its meditations on past glories. There is no link between them; they are foreign to each other and without continuity.

Beyond Jumla there are also temples of a more primitive type; open in front, with a straw roof supported on rough tree-trunks, they look like huts or the shrines of Assam or Polynesia. The artistic tradition of the Malla is dead.

Inside them crude wooden figures represent in awe-struck immobility the images of the donors, whole families in spell-bound vigil around the shapeless stones wherein is hidden the presence of divinity.

The civilization of the ancient stone-temple builders did not decline to this state of torpor by slow wasting or corruption, but was replaced by new migrations or impacts.

The *pandit* who accompanied me refused to call the religion of these people Hinduism, but defined it contemptuously as adoration of spirits and demons, *bhut*, treacherous and vindictive. The fear of invisible forces hovers around and menaces from every hill-top or from the branches of accursed trees on which coloured rags, hung there by prudent wayfarers, continue their exorcisms with every breath of wind.

Near Chumpithan a withered tree, on which rags of all colours fluttered and little bells like those used to tie round the necks of cows were hanging, seemed to be held in especial devotion. Devotion is perhaps not the most appropriate word, since fear was the sentiment that prompted the wayfarers to recite a prayer and to tie another piece of stuff to the withered branches before hastily going on their way. They told me that many years ago a woman did not want to be burned alive on her husband's funeral pyre, as was then the custom in these parts and in India. She was killed by the relatives of the dead man and from that moment became a *bhut* who would not pardon those who failed to propitiate her. Even more dangerous are the *bhut* who hover about the approaches to bridges or paths suspended in the void or on thin boards laid on piles and fixed into the rock-face of perpendicular cliffs where the path has no other means of ascent. Such places, in themselves filled with risk, are the most suitable for the *bhut* to give vent to their wrath; then the traveller must be even more cautious if he does not wish the demon to seize him. The bridge at Kotbara is one of the most feared, since there lives the spirit of a Brahman who committed suicide in this place. No one would dare to set foot on this bridge after nightfall. Night is the kingdom of infinite possibilities when everything, losing its familiar outline and the individuality given to it by daylight, returns to the confusion of chaos.

To conclude; exploration in space has been transformed into exploration in time. For the first time in our knowledge there rises before us an empire which united Tibetan and Indian provinces under the twofold standard of Hinduism and Lamaism. We see its founders ascend the courses of the sacred rivers that flow down to replenish the Ganges, and then stop on the shores of the Brahma Lake and near the foothills of the mountains of Shiva, Manasarovar and Kailasa, where today as formerly the pilgrims gather together from all parts of India to raise in that sublime beauty their supplications to the inaccessible divinities.

In 1931, continuing my trans-Himalayan exploration undertaken in 1926, I brought to light the events of western Tibet as revealed by its temples. Now, almost at the conclusion of more than thirty years of travel, in which I have walked more than twelve thousand miles over the Roof of the World, and after having crossed and recrossed the Himalayas in all directions and many times left their highest peaks behind me, the story has ended almost where it began only a short way from the same lake and the same mountain that saw me too (when for the first time it appeared to me wrapped in its luminous transparency) bending my knee unwittingly with the pilgrims. For in the silent encounters of nature I sensed irresistibly a presence that made me feel both humble and exalted.

Descent to the Terai

Our journey now moves rapidly towards its close. But the way is still long and the worst part is still before us. On the summits of the passes, alongside the firs, the agave offers to the skies, like the prayer of a dying man, its first and last flower, and we see below the plain of India, level and mist-covered like a sea of stone. A leaden-coloured sun beats without splendour over the sinuous indolence of the rivers. The last orchids drip from the tired tree-trunks like a flicker of departing life. In vain the paths turn and twist among the villages; it is like crossing a desert. Whoever has not made ample provision must either steal or die of hunger, for they will not sell you even a fruit. The sun, though languishing, has still the force to make the whole terrain seem level.

Step by step as we descend, the danger of disease grows greater. Snakes begin to glide through the undergrowth by the edge of the track. But that is not the reason why the caravan men go more cautiously. One day I saw the man who led the march and who was acting as our guide standing upright on a rock at a turning in the road with hands raised in prayer. At his feet was a cobra with distended hood watching him threateningly. But he did not move and would have preferred to be bitten rather than kill it. The snake is a *naga*, a mysterious creature linked with the obscure forces of the underworld, which guards the treasures hidden in the womb of the earth and the springs which give it life; it is the symbol of Shiva, the sign of time that always renews itself. Between killing and being killed many would still choose the second alternative.

Lonely herms even here mark the road of conquest, which was the road of death for many; they can be found as far as Surkhet and even beyond, to be lost at last in the first scattered outposts of the Terai. But the misadventures of the journey were not yet over. At Surkhet the porters from Dullu refused to go any farther and this gave rise to fresh misgivings, since in these sparsely populated villages it is not easy to find another fifty porters willing to go with us as far as the frontier.

Furthermore we had advised the Nepalese authorities that we would return to India by way of Nepalganj and they had instructed the governor of that city to do all that he could to assist us. But as I have already said Nepal is the country of the unexpected and the only certainty in plans is the certainty of uncertainty.

At Surkhet too, when they heard talk of Nepalganj, they were horrified and obstinately refused a wage four or five times greater than the usual one. Nor were they wrong. Of what use is money when scarcely any man ever returns along that road? Up to the middle of December the Terai is closed, since malaria kills in a few days any man rash enough to venture there. The magistrate gave me to understand that even had the love of gain persuaded some of the waverers to defy the jungle, he would have felt bound to dissuade them from doing so. The reason for this refusal was that for another month—we were then at the end of November—the Terai allowed no one to pass; if I had decided to go on to Nepalganj, we would have been exposed for another fortnight in one of its worst areas. For almost nine months of the year to stop in the Terai is to risk death, as the soldiers of the East India Company learnt to their cost when they tried to invade Nepal by this route.

I had known of this terror; moreover I had not forgotten that a few days earlier we had found a man who had returned from the zone of pestilence dying by the roadside. I therefore chose another route which, without avoiding the Terai, reduced our stay in that dangerous area by some days.

Three types of illness, they say, afflict these places; firstly there is the *jar*, the fever, a contagion of milder form that is shown by shiverings and fever, above all at night. Quite another thing is the *aul*, which kills in a few weeks; but the most feared is the *shit*, which brings death in four or five days. The word *shit* means 'cold', and the people think that the disease is caused by the dense mist which rises from the earth at nightfall and envelops everything in a sticky and silent curtain. Everything is impregnated by it as by a cold sweat that dews the grass, the trees and the rocks, and which only the sun next morning can bit by bit dissolve.

Probably it is a question of a type of fever against which the travellers are unprotected as was then the case all over Nepal where, out of eight million inhabitants more than five million were said to be ill from malaria and kalazar (*Leishmaniosis donovani*) and where, save in the capital and in some other major centres, there was only the most modest medical assistance. But now things have begun to change; the World Health Organization has drawn up a much needed plan for improvement. Nepal has need, like many countries of Asia equally eager to make up for lost time, of hospitals and above all roads. Only those who know the methods of travel in Nepal and Tibet, the dangers of the paths and the primitive road system, can understand what a drawback this is for the development of the country. The progress it wishes to attain will remain a utopia if the road problem is not solved first of all.

Among the Taru in the realm of the wild beasts
The Terai is one of the largest jungles in India: its dense forests run like a girdle inside the southern frontiers of Nepal and act as a defence. The Indian plain stops abruptly at a barrier of thorns and undergrowth

which soon grows denser with trees of every kind. This barrier spreads little by little over a maze of hillocks, which quickly become hills and then ranges of mountains running in all directions, at first parallel to one another and then suddenly diverging and intersecting in a confusion of summits that look down on the green all-enveloping silences of the forest. Nepal is protected by this barrier furrowed by torrents and defiles; at more infrequent intervals the rivers flow slowly through, expanding without hindrance and seeming to forget the constriction of the stony valleys that they forced their way through in the impetus of their birth.

The Terai is the kingdom of the wild beasts; man enters there as a stranger and an enemy. Along the paths worn by the seasonal rains and not the footsteps of man one follows the prints of the elephants and the tigers which have preceded one during the night. By day everything is tense and silent; only a bird mourns solitary in the depths. The snakes, alarmed at the slightest sound, slither back into their holes. In the heavy air there is a sensual and deadly stirring, like the breathing of a living thing that is dying because of its too great prodigality.

But it must not be thought that because the Terai is unhealthy it is devoid of life; there is no place and no danger that can halt the migrations searching for fresh habitations. Even into such places one of the many races that make up the ethnic mosaic of Nepal found its way in ancient times; this race is the Taru, and it speaks a language which in its basic structure is not Indo-European.

The Taru is last on the long list of the peoples whom we met during our journey. No one knows exactly how many languages and dialects are spoken in Nepal, certainly several dozen. As well as the Ghurkas who governed the country after Prithivi Narayan (eighteenth century) there are the Newari, who were deprived by that king of all their power, the Gurung, the Magar, the Limbu, the Bhutia, the Kiranti, the Murmi and many others, divided and sub-divided into castes and sub-castes and groupings so numerous that the ethnographical study of Nepal, despite the many researches undertaken, is still one of the most complex in the world. The languages become modified and altered, fade into one another, borrow words and idioms. So it is that the Newari tongue of certain documents a century or so old is almost incomprehensible to present-day Newaris, whereas no single document is extant from some of the other peoples like the Kiranti even though in ancient times they held power enough in the vale of Kathmandu and were perhaps among the earliest peoples to inhabit it.

It has been said that the Taru should by now be immune to the pestilence that makes even a brief stay in the area dangerous to any other person. But this is far from true; centuries of experience have to a certain extent vaccinated them against the *aul*, but it is enough to look at them, with their swollen bellies on emaciated bodies, to realize that they too have not been spared. But they have not despaired, and with great toil and diligence have cleared broad oases of cultivation in the dense forest.

Every village is a self-contained unit, though, springing one from the other in the cleared forests and for reasons of common defence, they are near one another in the leafy ocean that hems them in on all sides. The terrors and the perils of the jungle are kept back by high palisades that encircle the houses to protect the inhabitants and their domestic animals from the nightly forays of the wild beasts.

Their houses are comfortable, unusually clean, and built in a manner that makes the summer heat more bearable; large rooms at each end of the house form a family meeting-place, a kitchen and a storehouse; in the central part are the bedrooms divided by a narrow passage. In one corner, very close to the kitchen, is the domestic chapel if one may so call a small square space surrounded by a low raised border, in the midst of which images of horses or elephants in terracotta keep watch over the libation bowls.

The religion of the Taru has no liturgical complications; it is the frank expression of the wonderment of a people thrust into the denseness of a hostile nature, shoulder to shoulder with the beasts, in a cohabitation that is often downright brotherhood. Man has not yet risen to a consciousness of his own superiority over the animal world and has no advantage over it; some animals, for reasons that often escape our logical understanding, seem to him imbued with an aura of divinity which exalts them over all other beings and therefore makes them worthy of reverence. First among these are the horse and the elephant, the former perhaps because of its docility, the second because of its strength. The only defence available to man is magic; spells, incantations, offerings and prohibitions guide and protect him.

The resistance of the Taru in face of the unrelenting inhumanity of nature and their familiarity with the terrors of the jungle have diffused among the nearby peoples who live outside the forest the belief that the Taru, and especially their women, are skilled in the arcane sciences. Thus the comfort in which they live is not credited to their industry but rather to the favour of those powers whom they know how to bend to their will.

The Taru are not content merely to build their houses

in a comfortable and spacious manner, such as is rarely to be found among peoples of their cultural level, but they also decorate them with great care. On the still damp outer walls they design in relief figures of animals and hunting scenes, well drawn and full of movement. The women spend much of the time that they have free from their labours in the fields in embroidering the brilliant bell-shaped skirts which stand out against their sunburnt bodies and on which glitter the reflections of silver coins.

At night they meet together for the dance, the only relaxation which they allow themselves. The whole village squats in a circle on the ground, around a small space left free for the dancer and her accompanist, who beats a big drum and underlines his song with the sound, the cadence of the steps and the swaying of his body. The song serves to excite the lithe movements of the dancer who sits on the ground, face covered with a veil, seemingly absorbed in her modesty; then, little by little, as if yielding to the appeal of the song, she rises slowly and begins to dance more and more gaily; her skirt traces shimmering circles and the flames of the fires and the torches are reflected from it in vivid colour, breaking through the darkness in bright flashes; as the rhythm changes to a more rapid beat, her head bends languidly on her neck, now right now left, and her hands, waving and gesturing, express her inner emotion in the silent language of the dance. This animation spreads also to the spectators, who sing in chorus and reply to the invitation of the voice and drum, taking up the song of the accompanist and beating their hands in cadence. This takes place almost every evening until late at night, but on more important occasions and especially on the nights of full moon or new moon the whole village takes an active part in the songs and dances; then it is no longer an entertainment but a rite. Primitive man is filled with wonder at the regularity of nature, at the continual, immutable repetition of the same events, at the ordered return of the planets and the seasons; that is the miracle which disturbs and affects him. Miracle is not the unforeseen, the unusual, the unexpected, but the perpetual certainty of the order of creation.

Now at last we are at the end. While we are cautiously threading our way through the denseness of the jungle we hear unexpectedly the whistle of a train. After four months of wandering inside a country so different from our own, this sudden return to the everyday world disturbs us. Perhaps the first withdrawal from things which have become familiar is difficult, but little by little new habits take the place of old ones. Solitude and change invoke in us the life of our ancestors. Man is a creature suspended between the future of which he knows nothing and the past which sleeps deep within his consciousness; but that past, as soon as it finds favourable circumstances, rises to the surface like water that gushes from the sub-soil when the earth is riven. Thus it was strange how, in the course of our journey, despite the labour, the risks and the sacrifices, the familiar world never seemed alive to us as if it had not had the time to solidify and to deposit its sediment. Perhaps the nomadism of ancient times is a natural and essential state of man; all the rest is a prison term separating us from our natural condition.

We arrived suddenly at Nishangara, a tiny station lost in the fringes of the forest. Our unexpected presence flabbergasted the officials and the people; the first reaction is always one of suspicion. Two days later a smoky little train loaded us for Lucknow whence an aircraft took us back to Kathmandu to fetch our luggage. Thus my sixth journey in Nepal came to an end. But I have only to close my eyes as I walk among my mountains for all the images to rise again fresh and living before me, and the places I have visited and the people I have met reappear one by one in a purity of light that shall never be extinguished while I live.

55. The great steles of Dullu, bearing the complete genealogy of the Malla kings.

58. *The caravan makes ready to wade the Beriganga.*

59. *Village granary on the Terai.*

60. *A Taru cart.*

The population of Nepal appears to be about eight millions. The country is situated between longitude 80° and 88° and latitude 26° and 30° and stretches over a large area south of the Himalayas. It borders on Tibet in the north and India in the south; on the east it touches Sikkim, from which it is separated by Kanchenjunga and the Singhalala chain, and on the west by Kumaon, the two countries being separated by the Kaliganga. Its present size is due to events which took place in the eighteenth and nineteenth centuries. It is not and never has been homogeneous in race or civilization. The peoples that inhabit it are very varied; first of all the Gurkhas, who claim Aryan descent, then the Bhutias in the north, Gurung, Limbu, Magar and above all Newari who established their hegemony after various vicissitudes in the highland valley of the Bagmati (a tributary of the Gandaki river) where the principal cities, including the capital Kathmandu, are situated, and Taru in the Terai. These people are in great part of Tibeto-Burmese stock. The discord and division into which they fell made the conquest of the whole country by the Gurkhas of Prithivi Narayan in the eighteenth century an easy one.

How history began in this valley we do not know; but according to tradition it was early settled by the Kirati, upon whom were superimposed migrations from India from the times of Asoka (third century B.C.), of whose empire this section of Nepal may have formed part. Only careful archaeological research can solve this problem. But

81

it is a fact that in the middle of the fourth century A.D. a dynasty belonging to the Licchavi family, well known since the times of Buddha, took possession of this part of the country. Their civilization was closely influenced by that of the Guptas who founded a great empire in India from the end of the third to the sixth century A.D.; their inscriptions are in Gupta characters, and their administration was in many ways similar to that of the Guptas, though preserving traditional customs and forms. Their original place-names were frequently non-Aryan; their religion was mainly Shivaist and their devotion and their rites were addressed to that particular form of Shiva called Pasupatti, who is still the protecting deity of the country. This valley, where Nepalese civilization developed, therefore, very soon fell culturally under the influence of India and has always remained subsidiary to it. For this reason the history of Nepal cannot be understood except in relation to that of India.

Buddhism, by the tolerance of the ruling classes, also prospered, though traces of Buddhism are scarce in the inscriptions which so far have come to light. In the seventh century a vassal prince took power into his own hands and founded the first dynasty known as the Thakurs but then, from half-way through the seventh century up to 1000 A.D., there is a great hiatus. There are no inscriptions and no coins and the only evidence for this long and shadowy period is that of the chronicles, which have very little historical value. The one thing certain is that during this interval, and specifically in 879, the Newari period began, which lasted until 1768. In the eleventh century the second Thakur dynasty was founded which, however, soon fell under the sovereignty of the Kings of Tirhut in India. Buddhism in the meantime continued to penetrate into Nepal, which for this very reason, being closely linked with the Buddhist universities of Bihar and Bengal and with the art-schools of those areas, was to act as a mediator between Buddhist India and Tibet, where Buddhism had acquired almost complete dominion. Nepal was to bring this task of mediation between Indian and Tibetan culture to perfection through the centuries; for a long time Nepal provided artists for the abbots or the Tibetan princes anxious to embellish with statues or frescoes the temples which they built, or to cast statues or copy early Buddhist manuscripts for the monasteries as long as that spiritual and literary fervour, which induced the monks to study Sanskrit and to translate into their own language the masterpieces of Buddhist ritualistic and dogmatic literature, continued to endure in Tibet. In 1200 A.D. Arimalla founded a new dynasty, that of the Malla; in their times, as a result of the Moslem invasion of India, the Kings of Tirhut who had never renounced their rights of sovereignty over Nepal were driven from their capital Simraon and entered Nepal. They occupied Bhatgaon and founded a state which survived until the middle of the fifteenth century. It was a troubled history with many ups and downs, even though all of them, because of the limited area in which they took place, were of modest proportions; one only of the Malla kings who ruled over the valley with the exception of Bhatgaon is worthy of special mention, Jayasthiti Malla (1380-1400 A.D.), since he succeeded in establishing a new and wise administration and in putting an end to the continuous and disastrous unrest among his people. But his work of unification did not last for long; in 1475 the Malla were divided into four states, each centred in its own city; three of these, Kathmandu, Bhatgaon and Patan, rivals and often at feud with one another, survived until

1768-9 when Prithivi Narayan put an end to their existence.

Notwithstanding this turbulence, which recalls a little that of the petty Italian *signorias*, in which the nobles played an active part, art and civilization flourished. The Newari, amongst whom Buddhism was widely diffused, knew how to educate their aesthetic sense and to produce works of value which, even though they did not always rise to the dignity of real works of art, none the less proved the existence in Nepal of one of the most outstanding bodies of craftsmen in the East. They naturally drew a great deal of their inspiration from the artistic tradition of India but none the less developed and clarified certain of their own ideas and were not insensible to influence from beyond the Himalayas, thereby conferring a special character both on their architecture and on their painting and sculpture. From the many temples overburdened with gilded decoration one gets the impression that the exaltation of faith could not have been expressed with so great a luxury if the country, despite its internal troubles, had not possessed considerable economic resources, due in great part to its trade with India and Tibet and also to the hinterland which extended into the highlands and the neighbouring valleys. But the rest of the country now contained within the present frontiers of Nepal went on living a life of its own. The Malla of whom I have spoken earlier in this book must not be confused with those who governed in the valley of Kathmandu in later times; they founded between the tenth and the thirteenth century a great empire which ruled over both Tibet and western Nepal. But they were Khasiyas and had no connection with the Mallas of India, of whom there is ample record in Buddhist literature. Infiltrations from India continued; they came mostly from south-central India and were mainly caused by the Moslem invasions, but in part also to the drive for expansion northward of the Indian dynasties, for example the Chalukya and their vassals. These newcomers speaking Aryan dialects replaced the native peoples of Tibeto-Burman stock as a feudal aristocracy and carved out modest little states for themselves in Nepalese territory; thus Nepal soon became divided into twenty-six petty kingdoms—the *chaubis raj*. One of these kings, Prithivi Narayan, moved down from his castle of Gurkha, invaded the valley and in 1769 imposed his iron rule on all three of the major cities, Kathmandu, Patan and Bhatgaon. Malla supremacy was at an end, the Newari were deprived of all their privileges and rights, and the language of the new state was the Gurkhali or Nepali, an Aryan language which was the speech of the ruling class. Not content with having subjected the valley to his rule, Prithivi Narayan inaugurated a policy of great expansion; he first of all extended his rule over the *chaubis raj* and then advanced towards that northern frontier zone which had been widely penetrated by lamaist civilization and where the mass of the people were Tibetan; Mustang (in Tibetan *glo* or *blo*), Charka etc. He then pushed eastward as far as Bhutan and westward into Kumaon whence, however, he was expelled by the intervention of another great kingdom, that of the Sikhs, which was just then being created in India under the leadership of Ranjit Singh, whose best generals were two Italians, Ventura and Avitabile. But a more serious situation was being created in the north where Gurkha policy was risky and ambitious; they declared war on Tibet and advanced far into the interior, destroying and sacking monasteries and villages. The Chinese then intervened and drove the Gurkhas back into their own territory, and in 1792 the Chinese armies came

85

within a day's march of Kathmandu. There was nothing left save to accept the peace terms which, as has been the centuries-old custom of the Chinese, included the imposition of a tribute, payable every three years, as a sign of the formal subjection of Nepal to the then Celestial Empire.

When the war was drawing to a close the Gurkhas followed the example of the Newari kings whom they had replaced and who, in moments of danger, had asked for aid from the British; but in the time of the Newaris the British had had no success and had been forced to retire in face of the violence of the Gurkhas (battle of Haripur 1767) and the disastrous consequences of the deadly malaria which makes life impossible for a great part of the year in the Terai. This time, therefore, when war had broken out with China and the Nepalese found themselves forced to retreat they reluctantly asked for the intervention of the British. The request was embarrassing for the British too, for though they were eager to enter into closer relations with Nepal they had no great wish at that time to come into conflict with China, in which they had begun to take a great interest. Thus Lord Cornwallis came to a compromise and sent Colonel Kirkpatrick to arrange a peace; but he arrived when the war was already over and the only fruit of his mission, which politically was of little use, was that he wrote a book which is still of the greatest value for the history of Nepal.

Mutual suspicion, Britain's desire to enter into closer relations with Nepal, and a series of frontier incidents provoked growing tension which led to the war of 1814; fought with varied fortunes, it ended by the defeat of the Gurkhas despite their brave and desperate resistance, which was however in vain because of the superiority of means at the disposal of their adversaries. This led to the peace of Sagauli in 1816 by which Nepal was limited more or less within her present frontiers, ceding Kumaon, Garhwal and a part of the Terai, and which established diplomatic relations with the East India Company and allowed British representatives to live in Kathmandu. This fresh defeat led to unrest and very severe disorders which lasted, after many struggles and conspiracies, until the coming on the scene of a strong man, Jang Bahadur (1846-1878), who became Prime Minister and took absolute power into his hands. This led to a complete reversal of affairs; the king henceforth became a simple figurehead divorced from public life but invested with a pompous religious veneration which ensured him the maximum formal respect but divested him of any real power. This was now centred in the hands of the Prime Ministers of the Rana family who assumed the title of Maharaja; this rank became hereditary in the Rana family and its exclusive privilege. The tension between the Newari and the Gurkhas increased; even the use of the Newari language was banned and the Gurkhali language was made obligatory. The greatest attention was paid to the formation of a strong army which exploited the military virtues and the fighting spirit of the Gurkhas. The rapprochement with Britain became closer; Nepal allowed the British to recruit Gurkha soldiers on her territory, with whom the British formed special regiments of which they made successful use in various wars or military actions in which they were employed. But on the other hand this recruiting produced considerable advantages for Nepal who did not fail to show her friendship for Britain from the outbreak of the Indian Mutiny in 1857 down to the World War.

The influence of Britain over Jang Bahadur was once more evident during the war against Tibet which Britain, then engaged in a contest with Russia over spheres of influence in Central Asia, wanted to keep free of any foreign influence whatsoever and to make a buffer state. The Nepalese profited from the Crimean War of 1854 and from the withdrawal of the Chinese garrisons to meet the threat of the Taiping rebellion, penetrated into Tibet and forced her by the Treaty of 1856 to pay an annual tribute of ten thousand rupees and to allow a Nepalese resident to stay in Lhasa to watch over the interests of the Nepalese merchants.

The greatest of the Ranas was Chandra Sham Sher, who gave a great impulse to the country and tried to improve Kathmandu and the neighbouring cities. He and the members of his family built huge palaces, but save for a few short-term measures they did nothing to relieve the living conditions of the people, to improve the road system or to provide for public works or health services. One of his laws, however, deserves special mention, namely that promulgated in 1926 abolishing slavery. From the viewpoint of foreign policy he was, at a time when relations between Britain and Russia were more than usually tense, generous in his aid to Colonel Younghusband's expedition, which reached Lhasa and led to an agreement whereby Tibet undertook not to cede any part of her territory to any foreign power or to permit any foreign activities within her frontiers. An agreement on these lines could not but find the Nepalese Prime Minister in willing accord with the British. It paved the way for the formal recognition of Nepalese independence by the British which took place in 1923.

A person of great importance and authority during the rule of the Ranas was the *Rajguru*, the spiritual director and state-counsellor, supreme moderator of the moral, social and religious life of Nepal. The institution of this office was the consequence of that special ethnic and religious situation existent in Nepal where there has never been any homogeneity; alongside the ancestral and primitive religious and social customs still existent in the less progressive areas, a numerous and ancient Buddhist community had prospered, while Hinduism which was dominant among the ruling classes had been trying little by little to impose its own moral code and above all its principle of caste division. But the very complexity of the ethnic components of Nepal and the variety of social and religious traditions, together with the existence of tribal organizations that differed from one part of the country to another, made the organization of the Nepalese people in a caste system more difficult and less rigid than in India proper. It was not possible to avoid intermingling, the infiltration of new elements and especially mixed marriages; this made the Nepalese castes far less closed and more elastic than those in India. Especially after the Gurkha domination an ever greater Hindu penetration was taking place before which Buddhism was retreating, though with concessions on both sides so that sometimes the points of contact between Buddhism and Shivaism were so many and of such a nature as almost to amount to a symbiosis.

The Ranas had a peculiar rule of succession; on the death of the reigning Rana the power passed to his brothers and then to the eldest son of the eldest brother. But despite its good relations with Britain Nepal remained a closed and suspicious country. No one entered it save under suspicion and under surveillance. Meanwhile in India affairs were moving slowly but fatefully; young Nepalese could not remain indifferent to those continual movements which were paving the way for the independence of India. While attending Indian universities they had every opportunity of comparing the extreme backwardness in which the people were kept in their own country with the greater freedom of expression allowed in India, and above all the continuing development of India: railways, roads, hospitals and the like. Nepal remained practically a feudal country, so cut off from the world that to get there the traveller had to descend at the narrow-gauge railhead at Amlekganj, take a car for a few miles and then continue for two days on foot, in a litter or on horseback to Kathmandu, crossing two passes on the way.

The Prajaparishat, or People's Party, was formed in 1938 with the help of the Socialist Party of Bihar and led to the first skirmishes, to which the Ranas replied with repressive measures; but from then on the inevitability of a new dispensation was clearly to be seen. The delusion of the many tens of thousands of soldiers provided by Nepal for the British and who had now returned to their country fresh from their impression of a quite different sort of world, the influence of the political movements astir in India upon the exiles or political refugees, and the reactions of the Ranas themselves, all led to the formation of the Nepalese National Congress inaugurated at Calcutta in 1946 and supported financially by Subarna Sham Sher, an illegitimate brother of Padma Sham Sher whom the Ranas, anxious to preserve the succession, had forced to seek refuge in India, even though they had agreed that illegitimate sons could take part in the succession.

The situation soon became even more paradoxical; the last Rana, Mohan Sham Sher, who was deeply conservative but forced by the pressure of events to adapt himself reluctantly to the new conditions, remained slavishly devoted to the interests and prestige of his family; the members of the Congress, eager to get on the bandwagon, squabbled among themselves for leading places, causing a split in the Congress itself. The invasion of

Tibet by the Chinese increased the anxiety of India and Nepal, especially when it became known that on some Chinese maps Nepal was shown as Chinese territory. Mohan Sham Sher, who had already offered his aid to India in the Hyderabad annexation crisis, though not unaware that Nepalese independence movements were looked on with favour and encouraged in India, hastened to Delhi to sign a Treaty of Friendship by which Nepalese sovereignty was guaranteed. And it was by Indian insistence that Mohan Sham Sher decided to nominate a parliament which met at Kathmandu on September 22nd, 1951, but had no practical result. Tension became even greater; the fires smouldered. King Tribhuvana thought the moment ripe to restore its lost power to the dynasty from which he was descended. He took refuge in the Indian Embassy and was granted asylum. In vain Mohan Sham Sher nominated his son, who was scarcely three years old, as king. Tribhuvana sought safety in India where he fled in an Indian aeroplane; the situation gained momentum. An insurrection stirred up by the Congress broke out in Nepal; when the troops joined the insurgents, Mohan Sham Sher was forced to yield. Tribhuvana returned to Kathmandu where a Coalition Cabinet was formed, with the Rana, Mohan Sham Sher, as President. It was a solution that could not satisfy either side. The Congress insisted that a cabinet be formed which meant a clean break with the old regime. In November 1951 Mohan Sham Sher resigned and took refuge in India. The King entrusted the President of the Nepalese Congress, M. P. Koirala, to form a new cabinet made up of eight members of the Congress itself and four independents. But despite all this, the country had not yet attained stability; the transition from a feudal regime to a regime of democratic liberty had been too sudden. In the minds of these political leaders lust for power and the cupidity of easy gains were added to the conviction that they were serving their country; they aimed at surrounding themselves by a vast horde of hangers-on, and at acquiring privileges or positions of prestige. Personal interests took precedence over the welfare of the people. The ruling class had not yet been created, because it had had neither the time nor the favourable conditions in which to develop. Political life degenerated for the most part into squabbles, rivalries and cabals which led to an unstable situation of little value to the country. From 1950 to 1956 there were five ministries, with an interval of direct rule by the Crown-prince Mahendra when his father went to Europe for a cure. On his father's death Mahendra was forced by the insistence of the politicians to form a new cabinet with Tanka Prasad, President of the Prajaparishat, as Prime Minister.

The Koirala brothers then began to quarrel among themselves, leading to fresh divisions; between '55 and '57 there were two more ministries; Doctor K. I. Singh, who had been three years in China and was suspected of being a communist, unexpectedly became Prime Minister. But he had to resign in 1957 and the power once again passed into the hands of the king. The decision forced upon the king by the dissensions between the politicians provoked violent protests and a Satyagraha movement of Gandhian type that peremptorily demanded general elections to be held within six months. The demonstrations went on until the king announced that the elections would be held in February, 1959.

On February 12th, 1959, King Mahendra promulgated the proposed constitution; but already in November 1958 he had appointed a Consultative Assembly of eighty-five members which was, however, immediately dissolved. The elections began on February

18th and closed at the end of April without incident, but out of an electorate of 4,120,000 only 45% appeared at the polls. This was not to be wondered at, seeing that about 90% of the people were illiterate.

There were six parties in the lists, including the communist party. The Nepalese Congress, of moderate socialist tendencies, whose president was B. P. Koirala, won by an enormous majority. Koirala became Prime Minister. In these elections several leaders who had taken a prominent part in the political life of the country were defeated, including some who had already been Prime Minister: Dr K. L. Singh, Dr Regmi and Tanka Prasad.

All this did not essentially change the psychological situation or the immature democracy of which I have spoken. Furthermore, Nepal was now to find herself the catspaw of two great neighbours: China and India. The former tried to extend her influence south of the Himalayas, drawing every advantage from the sympathy felt for her among many elements of the Newari people; the latter was not disposed to tolerate foreign activities in a nation where her own interests were vital and where she had begun to sink much capital in order to improve its economic and industrial development. Nepal was forced to take part in the current of neutralism by signing a Treaty of Friendship with China. Chou-en-Lai went to Kathmandu and Koirala returned the visit. The treaty of 1856 by which the Nepalese enjoyed extra-territorial rights in Tibet and which had stipulated an annual, even if purely formal, tribute was abrogated in 1956. China offered Nepal a large loan but, in order not to offend the susceptibilities of India which was much preoccupied by this move, did not insist on the despatch of technicians.

93

When Koirala went to Peking an agreement was reached on the demarcation of the frontiers between Nepal and Tibet, at a time when the great dispute, which has not yet been settled, between India and China about the Sino-Indian frontier had already commenced. In 1959 the Soviet Union offered six million dollars and China five million for a three-year period. Russia built a sugar refinery, a tobacco factory and hydro-electric power stations. India contributed twenty million dollars to aid the Nepalese second five-year plan for the five-year period 1956-61. American aid was also substantial.

So ended the times of seclusion. Nepal has now entered international life and cannot withdraw from the consequences of her historical maturity. She has become a member of the FAO, of UNESCO, of the United Nations (from 1956) and of the International Postal Union. Whereas previously she had had diplomatic relations only with Tibet (naturally suspended after that country had passed under Chinese control), with Great Britain and with India, she has today extended her relations to the major powers, from the United States to France and from the Soviet Union to China, and recently even to Italy.

In a country where malaria and black-fever are still widespread, medical aid is still in its infancy despite the intervention of the World Health Organization. Almost everything has still to be done in the field of education; the insufficient and inadequate schools, many of them private, can provide only an approximation of culture; secondary schools are few and there is a scarcity of teachers. The young men who finish at the colleges at Kathmandu go to Lucknow, Benares or Calcutta to complete their studies. A national university is now being founded with foreign aid; but the task is a very hard one, because great resources, much equipment and above all a body of teachers worthy of the task awaiting them, are necessary.

Nepal is now trying to find her own road. In December, 1960, the King unexpectedly arrested all the members of the Cabinet. There was talk of undue docility by Koirala to Indian demands and it is also said that the conflict between the King and the Prime Minister had been going on for some time, inasmuch as the latter wanted to reduce even more the nominal power of the king. The fact is that Nepal has now more or less returned to a controlled regime, repressive laws have been passed, and many liberties curtailed.

This sudden return to a situation that for the time being annuls so many years of struggle for liberty was disapproved of by the Indian press and by Nehru himself. There is no doubt that by these measures Nepal has taken a step backwards; a repressive regime may provoke a revival of the left-wing currents capable of rallying all the malcontents. Various movements have been noticeable in all parts of the country.

Nepal is therefore in a period of expectation and crisis. In fact in Nepal, as in other oriental countries, democracy has for the moment failed; it has failed because of the immaturity of the leaders, because of the unforeseen superimposition of badly digested ideas on a society not yet unified, in which diverse races, languages and interests rival one another. Up to a few years ago she was a feudal country and it is therefore difficult for her to achieve the customs of the West in one bound. Some more time will be needed and some more work will have to be undertaken to improve the way of life, education, hygiene and communications before there dawns that political consciousness, that spirit of tolerance and disinterestedness, without which the political classes rather than helping their people bring them to ruin.

THE END